# Crashing the Dollar

Also by
**Craig R. Smith**

*Rediscovering Gold in the 21st Century:*
*The Complete Guide to the Next Gold Rush*

*Black Gold Stranglehold: The Myth*
*of Scarcity and the Politics of Oil*
(co-authored with Jerome R. Corsi)

Also by
Lowell Ponte
*The Cooling*

# Crashing the Dollar

## How to Survive a Global Currency Collapse

## Craig R. Smith

Swiss America
and Lowell Ponte

Foreword by Pat Boone

# Crashing the Dollar:
# How to Survive a Global Currency Collapse

## Publisher
Idea Factory Press - President, David M. Bradshaw
13232 N. 1st Avenue, Phoenix, AZ 85029 USA
Contact: phone (602) 918-3296 or
email ideaman@myideafactory.net

Cover art by Linda Daly, Dalybread.com
Based on a design concept by Lowell Ponte
Copy editing by Ellen Ponte

Library of Congress Data
**ISBN Number 978-0-9711482-1-5**
First Edition, October 2010

Updates and book reviews posted @
crashingthedollar.com

# Table of Contents

# Dedication

To my wonderful wife and best friend
Melissa Smith, who makes me better
each day and raised our daughters
Holly and Katie to love the Lord
with all their hearts.
Also to my Pastor Tommy Barnett,
who taught me that doing the right thing
is always the right thing to do,
and to always hold onto the vision.

# Foreword
## by Pat Boone

We used to say that a healthy person was "sound as a dollar."

Today the U.S. Dollar is not so healthy, and its decline is making us not so wealthy.

When we read that gold has gone to $1,300 per ounce, this means that it now takes 1,300 dollars to buy the same amount of gold that cost $35 when I was a kid.

Craig Smith, the founder of Swiss America, has warned for three decades that this weakening of the dollar was underway.

In this new book, Craig and former *Reader's Digest* Roving Editor Lowell Ponte explain why the dollar keeps falling and could soon crash.

Craig's trusted guidance helped me and my family, and thousands of others, protect our savings from the dollar's continuing decline in value.

In this eye-opening book, Craig and Lowell show what a crash of the dollar and other currencies would be like. They tell how America can avoid this economic disaster. They explain how you and your family, by preparing now, can survive, thrive, and even prosper during a collapse of the dollar.

Presidents of both major parties put an end to what America's Founders specified in our Constitution: a dollar as good as gold, the standard for honest money set forth in the Bible.

Because the paper dollar is now worth little more than politician promises, Americans face rising prices and sinking values. This book can help restore fundamental values we need to restore America. Take it to heart.

*Pat*

# Introduction

The United States is digging the biggest economic hole in human history.

This hole of debt is now so deep that, if you listen carefully, you can hear the voices of Chinese creditors asking one another if they will ever get back the $900 billion they have lent to us.

This hole of debt is so wide that it threatens to collapse the foundations not only of the U.S. Dollar and economy but also of other major currencies and economies around the world.

The global danger from this is so dire that even formerly free-spending European welfare states are responding with austerity measures and huge government spending cuts.

At the summer 2010 gathering of G-20 nations, Germany, the United Kingdom and other American allies urged President Barack Obama to join them in reducing spending.

President Obama refused. He instead has chosen to steer the United States in the opposite direction, away from austerity, time-proven prudence and government belt-tightening.

This is ironic because Mr. Obama and the congressional leaders of his party have been moving as fast as they can to remake the United States in the image of high-tax Eurosocialist cradle-to-grave (or should we say abortion-to-euthanasia-for-granny?) welfare states.

At the same time Obamacrats are moving America to the left, several of the biggest European countries, seeing the error of their past ways, are moving right. They are now shrinking socialist aspects of their societies, reducing government spending and the tax burden on their citizens and companies, and moving towards free enterprise.

## Money From Nowhere

Mr. Obama has said that he plans, in effect, to tax and spend America back to prosperity with yet more trillions of dollars – with more than four of every ten of them borrowed – in stimulus funding.

Economists are concerned about this for many reasons:

One is that this risky policy has never before been attempted on so large a scale, with the economy of the entire planet and the well-being – even the survival – of billions of people at stake if Obamanomics fails.

Another is that such redistribution of wealth is unjust, immoral, riddled with Chicago-style corruption, and inefficient. After destroying a society's wealth, it redistributes poverty – but not equally; government-favored fat cats will get fatter.

But the most immediate reason economists are concerned about Mr. Obama's policies is that the United States is already bankrupt.

We have no more money to spend, and even if government expropriated every penny earned or owned by the rich, this would not provide enough to bankroll the ambitious agenda of Obamanomics.

We no longer have enough genuine wealth to buy our way out of the trap of debt that we continue to dig deeper and wider every day.

Few Americans fully understand where we are, how we got here, how today's economic crisis puts humankind's future at risk, and how with the information in this book individuals can survive and even thrive after the dollar crash and world economic system cave-in that is coming.

## Go Ask Alice

Warning: what you will discover by reading this book is disturbing, even frightening.

To paraphrase the movie "The Matrix," if you prefer not to know the truth, put this book down now and you will awaken tomorrow morning to the usual bewildered view of a mysterious world economy.

If you read this book, you will never again be able to see the world in that old way.

Keep reading and you will discover, level after level, just how deep the Obamanomics rabbit hole goes, and how this is key to President Obama's apparent master plan for what he calls a "fundamental transformation" of America.

President Obama has only one way he can carry out his big spending plans.

Because the United States lacks the money needed to pay our debts, the United States and its Federal Reserve Board will simply print more.

Lots more.

Mr. Obama apparently intends to create enough paper money to build an escape ramp out of the debt hole that is devouring us, and perhaps enough to fill the hole completely.

Does this sound crazy?

Governments have done this before, and in this process that economists call "monetizing the debt" have almost always crashed their own currency and economy.

Despite – or perhaps because of – this risk of fatally crashing the dollar, President Obama's printing of an almost-limitless supply of money out of thin air has already begun.

In 2009 the U.S. monetary base effectively doubled, and this is only the beginning.

The amount of such fiat money – a term economists use to describe money whose only value comes from a government command, a fiat – needed to pay America's already-existing debts is literally astronomically large.

## Buy Me to the Moon

$4.4 Trillion is a lot of money.

A tightly-packed stack of 4.4 Trillion $1 bills would reach from the Earth to the moon 238,857 miles away.

This stack of money would then continue for an additional 59,753 miles, enough to travel around Earth's equator 2.4 times.

Since 2007, when Democrats took control of the U.S. Senate and House of Representatives, in a mere 31 months the Congress increased the Federal Government's 10-year spending baseline by more than $4.4 Trillion.

Congress has no revenue to pay for this additional spending. The Federal Government already borrows 41 cents of every dollar it spends.

By August 2010 Uncle Sam had already run up on this year's unpaid bar tab, our annual deficit, more than $1.47 Trillion so that politicians could stay intoxicated with ideological power and give vast stimulative spending to their cronies and campaign contributors and to buy votes.

The rest of us will sooner or later be paying the government's bills, of course, in one way or another. $4.4 Trillion is equivalent to more than $57,000 for every family of four in America.

Since only approximately 53 percent of us actually pay federal income tax, you should figure that you and your children and grandchildren will be paying at least $110,000 in today's dollars in taxes, higher prices, lost opportunities and social deterioration just for this $4.4 Trillion spending spree.

The total price we will pay for Obamanomics, however, will be immeasurably higher than this.

President Obama, his party, and his predecessors of both parties have done more than loot America's piggy bank.

They have broken the bank and the U.S. Dollar itself, as will soon be evident to everyone.

They have wounded our national currency so badly that it will almost certainly die.

Because of this, the world economic system built on the dollar is already beginning to tremble.

## The Debt Clock

Unable to raise adequate taxes, and unwilling to cut their unsustainable welfare state, Mr. Obama and his zealous Democratic lawmakers have already begun to monetize the debts and obligations that generations of politicians of both parties have run up – total debts, obligations and liabilities in excess of $112 Trillion.

Such things have happened before in other countries.

But could hyperinflation strike the United States?

I am old enough to remember when a "penny postcard" cost only two cents. Today it costs 28 cents, a 1400% increase since my childhood.

Are you old enough to remember when a billion – a thousand million – dollars seemed to be an unimaginably large amount?

Can you remember when President Richard Nixon nearly went apoplectic upon learning that America had an imbalance of trade, a deficit in our buying over selling with the world, of $4 billion per year?

Today just our trade deficit by itself in the world marketplace runs approximately $4 billion every 3.8 days, and we think nothing of this outpouring of our national wealth – the capital in our capitalism – our financial lifeblood bleeding away as we import that much more than we export.

We gradually grew comfortable, or at least numb, with our government measuring its spending in billions of dollars.

But now lawmakers and President Obama speak casually of spending and indebtedness that run to trillions – thousands of billions – of dollars.

And in the inner chambers of government, a new word is already being whispered – Quadrillion – a thousand thousand billion dollars, a $1 followed by 15 zeroes! – as the amount of debt risk we unwittingly may already have taken on.

In 2009 the keepers of our National Debt Clock on Sixth Avenue in New York City had to shut it down briefly. The problem: America's debt is now piling up so fast that their original financial doomsday clock contained too few digits.

They had to add new spaces for more zeroes.

This is the fourth time since its original installation in 1989 that the debt clock has had to be modified to display more numbers. This fact by itself suggests how big a growing national debt problem we face.

The debt clock's new incarnation can display debt of up to One Quadrillion dollars.

"I will show you fear in a handful of dust," wrote T.S. Eliot in his 1922 poem "The Wasteland," written near the height of the post-World

War I Weimar hyperinflation that was destroying traditional German faith and values, and sowing the seeds that soon would produce monsters.

Take a look at the Debt Clock on the Internet (http://www.usdebtclock.org) and you will see fear in a handful of ever-increasing numbers.

This clock has a message: Time for America as we have known and loved it is rapidly running out.

## You Can Be a Trillionaire

The Robert Mugabe Marxist regime in Zimbabwe paid its bills by printing unlimited national currency on government presses. This so devalued the nation's money that its latest paper fiat currency is the $100 Trillion Zimbabwe Dollar note.

When first issued in 2008, these bills could be bought internationally with a typical asking price of $30 U.S.

In September 2010, on Ebay they were offered at 50 for $89, a cost of $1.78 U.S. for a $100 Trillion Zimbabwean Dollar note.

Before 2009 ended, with the BBC reporting that consumer prices were doubling daily, the Government of Zimbabwe ceased printing and allowed its people – 80 percent of whom are unemployed – to buy and sell with foreign currency, especially U.S. Dollars.

Much the same occurred in Germany after World War I under a Weimar Republic government that ideologically and morally was chillingly similar to the Obama Administration and today's left-liberal Democrat-dominated Congress.

## When the Dollar Dies

But what we now face is far worse than one or another nation's money dying in a blaze of hyperinflation.

The U.S. Dollar is the world's "reserve currency," the stabilizer that other nations, large and small, stockpile in their own central banks as backing for their currencies. The U.S. Dollar is what ordinary people around the world hide in their home mattresses for use in case politicians make their local money worthless.

This is what Mr. Obama, his ruling party, and his predecessors, both Republicans and Democrats, have been debasing and destroying.

If the U.S. Dollar dies, a domino effect of other major currencies falling around the world would likely follow. The entire global system of money and credit could collapse, with terrifying consequences especially for the poor – as more of us join the ranks of the poor every day.

Mr. Obama could become the President who will put his boot on the corpse of the U.S. Dollar and deliver the eulogy at its funeral.

Part of this book is a travel guide to prepare you to live the next ten years of your life in a new Weimar hyperinflation collapse. You can learn which landmarks to watch for, what mistakes to avoid, and how to prepare so your family can survive and thrive in this very different world.

## The Seed

As the dollar weakens, any new attack or crisis might be the straw that breaks our national currency's back. This would bring down the curtain on a world in which the United States has for a century been the planet's civilizing Superpower and greatest hope, and the U.S. Dollar was the world's most reliable paper currency.

If American power collapses, who or what will be able to continue America's role holding back a new Dark Age shaped by Naziism, Communism, or radical Islamist terrorism?

We are heading into an "unusually uncertain" future – to use Federal Reserve Board chair Ben Bernanke's description of today's American economy.

This future might end in disintegration, collapse and war or, if we steer by the right star, could become the dawn of a new Golden Age where even dark clouds have gold and silver linings.

We are descended from pioneers and entrepreneurs who dared and overcame severe challenges to build a better world.

We are the children who carry their seed, and in us their American dreams can yet survive and succeed.

We have reason to be optimistic because, as President Ronald Reagan reminded us, we are Americans.

Fasten your seatbelt, dear reader. You are about to take an amazing ride.

Craig R. Smith

# Part One
# The Money Pit

# Chapter One
# Inflatable America

*"Paper is poverty.... It is only
the ghost of money,
and not money itself."*

**– Thomas Jefferson
Letter to Edward Carrington, 1788**

"What we didn't realize was just how large an economic nightmare lay before the new President and the American people," said Christina Romer, then still chair of President Barack Obama's Council of Economic Advisers.

Strong political action, she said, narrowly saved the United States from "a second Great Depression....the specter of a cataclysmic economic meltdown."

Thomas Jefferson would recognize this specter Romer sees haunting America's current economic nightmare. It is the ghost of the U.S. Dollar.

After hearing Dr. Romer's September 1, 2010, farewell luncheon speech, Washington Post staff writer Dana Milbank summed up what she said:

"She had no idea how bad the economic collapse would be. She still doesn't understand exactly why it was so bad. The response to the collapse was inadequate. And she doesn't have much of an idea about how to fix things."

"What she did have," Milbank continued, "was a binder full of scary descriptions and warnings....'Terrible recession....Incredibly searing.... Dramatically below trend....Suffering terribly....Risk of making high unemployment permanent....Economic nightmare.'

"Anybody want dessert?"

Dr. Romer, truth be told, knows perfectly well what is causing today's Great Recession and how to fix it.  She knows that nothing really has been fixed, that our nation remains on the cliff-edge of a fatal fall, and that the stimulus spending of President Obama not only failed to remedy our economy's sickness, but also made things worse.

She knows where the economy is now headed because President Obama is, for ideological reasons, unwilling to use historically-proven free market remedies.

To speak such politically inconvenient truths would harm her liberal team in upcoming partisan political and culture war battles, and especially in November's midterm elections.

Instead, President Obama's chief economic advisor spoke loudly with her feet by leaving his Administration before the much bigger coming disaster arrives.

Other key members of Mr. Obama's economic team – Office of Management and Budget director Peter Orszag and head of the National Economic Council Lawrence Summers – have likewise rushed to exit this sinking ship.

And in September 2010 Secretary of State Hillary Clinton warned that America's enormous and growing debt projects to the world a "message of weakness."  It "undermines our capacity to act in our own interest," Secretary Clinton said, "and it does constrain us where constraint may be undesirable."

To understand what is coming and why, and the roots of the world's current intertwined money-banking-housing crises, we need to look back almost four decades into the past to a single decision.

To paraphrase President Obama's spiritual mentor Dr. Jeremiah Wright, ever since that decision its chickens have been coming home to roost in ever-enlarging crises.

## Fateful Decision

"If historians searched for the precise date on which America's singular dominance of the world's economy ended, they might settle on August 15, 1971," wrote investigative journalist William Greider in his 1987 book *Secrets of the Temple: How the Federal Reserve Runs the Country.*

On that day Republican President Richard Nixon issued an Executive Order closing the "gold window" through which foreign central banks – in effect, foreign governments we favored – were able to exchange $35 in American currency for one Troy ounce of gold.

By this action, Mr. Nixon ended the central element of the 1944-45 Bretton Woods agreement among major Free World countries – that the United States guaranteed they could exchange U.S. Dollars for a fixed amount of gold (set from 1933 until 1971 at $35 per ounce).

Under Bretton Woods, friendly nations could peg their currency value to the dollar with assurance, knowing that the dollar had the stability of being pegged to gold in world trade and finance.

With a single unexpected blow, President Nixon severed this last tie that had anchored the Free World's currencies and economic system. At the time he declared that this change was temporary, but it remains today.

Ever since his action, each major currency – the dollar included – has had to sink or float in the often-turbulent seas of the global marketplace. Each has established its own independent value.

## Murdering the Dollar

One could say that President Nixon murdered the U.S. Dollar. He killed America's gold-standard currency and replaced it with a look-alike impostor fiat currency that has no guaranteed convertibility to anything by anybody – except debt, a specter that cannot be tasted, touched or smelled, but that can be perceived in the devastating damage it can cause.

One could, of course, also argue that the deceased pre-1971 dollar was also an impostor which replaced dollars that ordinary people, not only central banks, could convert into a government-guaranteed quantity of silver, the "poor man's gold" advocated as money by populist-progressives such as William Jennings Bryan.

Democratic President Lyndon Baines Johnson slammed shut the window for Silver Certificate conversion to silver dollars in March 1964 and terminated all redemption of dollars for silver on June 24, 1968, killing what Americans had relied on as their dollar.

President Johnson was escalating his martyred predecessor's war against communists in Vietnam, where Democratic President John F. Kennedy had committed the first 16,000 armed American troops into combat.

At the same time that Mr. Johnson was pursuing a guns-and-butter policy vis-a-vis this war, he also was building his costly Great Society welfare state at home.

By the early 1960s silver had reached a market value of $1.27, and people and nations rushed to reap a profit by converting their silver certificate dollars into the more precious metal. Mr. Johnson acted to halt this drain on U.S. silver reserves.

"The world supply of gold is insufficient to make the present system workable," said President Johnson in 1967.

That system was the last remnant of the dollar gold standard that Democratic President Franklin Delano Roosevelt eliminated in 1933 by Executive Order. He made it illegal for American citizens to own gold bullion without government permission.

President Nixon reluctantly agreed with LBJ because the U.S. gold reserves stored in Fort Knox were rapidly shrinking.

"By 1971," wrote Greider, "foreign financial institutions had amassed dollar claims totaling $36 billion – double the $18 billion in gold reserves the United States still held for international convertibility.

"If the President let events play out," wrote Greider, "the guarantor of world monetary order – the American government – would soon find its own storehouse empty. Its guarantee to the world would become meaningless by default."

Mr. Nixon shut the last dollar convertibility window for gold, just as Mr. Johnson did for silver. But did President Nixon act quickly enough?

Today Fort Knox's gold supply is under the control of the Federal Reserve Board, a private consortium of banks. The Fed is resisting and delaying a long-sought court order that it submit to at least a partial audit.

The Obama Administration and Democratic majority leaders in Congress have blocked legislation by Rep. Ron Paul (R.-Texas) that would require an independent audit to determine how much gold remains in Fort Knox.

## Golden Handcuffs

One of the greatest virtues of a gold standard is that it constrains government spending.

Most politicians always want to spend more, especially when they have a war to fight or new plans to bankroll. If they could simply print any amount of money they wished, their wishes would expand without limit.

But when each printed dollar is convertible to gold, this (at least in theory) means that a lawmaker or president can print only as much paper currency as the government has gold to redeem. This link turns gold into golden handcuffs on politicians.

This is an integral part of what America's Founders intended, as

Thomas Jefferson expressed by saying of power-hungry politicians that we should "bind them down with the chains of the Constitution."

The gold standard is therefore the friend of all who save money and want it to retain its value, of all who want their dollars to be an honest and reliable medium of exchange, and of taxpayers who, like America's Founders, want a limited and frugal government.

This, of course, is why so many of today's politicians hate the gold standard.

## Beyond Redemption

Presidents Johnson and Nixon – or, to be technical, the Federal Reserve Board whose chairman is appointed and re-appointed by presidents – ran far more paper money off government printing presses than the U.S. had gold or silver to redeem.

Shortly after Nixon terminated dollar-to-gold convertibility that had been fixed at $35, gold hit a market price of $72 per ounce.

We have been taught to say "gold's price rose" when we see stories of gold above $1,300 per ounce, but we can choose another, clearer way of thinking about this.

Gold has been the standard of human money for 5,000 years. It is the yardstick by which the value of paper money is measured, not the other way around.

The same amount of gold that 100 years ago could buy you a thousand board-feet of lumber, or a ton of coal, or a handsome horse will usually buy those same things today.

An ounce of gold will let you purchase an excellent man's suit, and that same ounce of gold 2,000 years ago in ancient Rome could buy an excellent toga.

Gold, in other words, does not change or "go up in value." What changes is the value of unreliable things, like paper fiat dollars, relative to gold.

When business reporters tell you that "gold has risen to $1,300 per ounce," what they actually mean is that the paper dollar has lost value, and it now requires 1,300 dollars to buy one ounce of gold.

When the dollar was anchored to gold's standard, the dollar retained its value.

But after 1971, when the golden handcuffs were removed from politicians in Washington, D.C., they began printing paper dollars out of thin air.

The power of politicians, however, has natural limits. They cannot outlaw gravity, and they cannot repeal the law of supply and demand.

In the marketplace, dollars are merely another commodity like potatoes or wheat.

When politicians double the supply of paper dollars to give themselves money to spend, this eventually reduces the demand for now-less-scarce dollars more or less by half, just as doubling the supply of potatoes would lead to lower potato prices.

This potentially devalues each and every dollar, including the ones you have earned and saved in your mattress. Public confidence in the worth of a dollar is a key factor in its value. As this confidence leaks away, the dollar's purchasing power sinks like a child's balloon as its helium leaks away. This leaves every dollar able to buy fewer potatoes than it previously could.

In 1890, one U.S. Dollar was an average lumberjack's daily pay in Minnesota. With one dollar, however, a worker then could buy 10 pounds of flour, two pounds of round steak, two quarts of milk, and 20 pounds of potatoes.

Economists call the devaluation of money by printing more of it inflation.

Some of the consequences inflation can unleash are as predictable as a sunset. Others are unanticipated consequences and can bring surprising ghosts, nightmares and destruction.

## Oiling the Money Machine

The U.S. Dollar that President Nixon killed was not an ordinary currency, and its murder started a chain reaction that continues to influence many of today's crises.

The Bretton Woods agreement had cemented the dollar's status as the Free World's "reserve currency."

This means that oil, for example, gets purchased internationally using U.S. dollars as the global medium of exchange.

When President Nixon cut the dollar loose from its gold anchor and began freely to print money, the dollar began – and to this day continues – to lose value.

Among those most troubled by this was OPEC, the Organization of Petroleum Exporting Countries, whose members saw their dollars rapidly losing value. Within months they struck back by raising oil prices.

"The OPEC price escalation was a direct and logical response to Nixon's fateful decision," wrote Greider. "Oil traded worldwide in dollars and if the United States was going to permit a free fall in the dollar's value, that meant the oil-producing nations would receive less and less real value for the commodity."

In early 1973 America could buy all the Saudi Arabian light sweet crude oil we desired for as little as $1 per barrel.

[ Scientists since then have found evidence that oil is not a "fossil fuel," but is created in vast amounts by another process deep inside the Earth. Oil may exist in huge abundance and could be made available today at pre-1971 Saudi prices. To learn more about this, see the widely-discussed 2005 book *Black Gold Stranglehold: The Myth of Scarcity and the Politics of Oil* by Jerome R. Corsi and Craig R. Smith, available from Swiss America or Amazon.com. ]

In summer 1973 a driver could find premium gasoline for 28 cents per gallon in Houston and 38 cents per gallon in Boston. One could find gas stations that retained the disappearing tradition of washing customer windshields, checking engine fluids, and throwing in a set of handsome free beverage glasses with each fill-up.

Americans found it cheap and easy to take Sunday drives and long vacation trips by automobile.

In summer 1973, an American could drive a Toyota Corolla from Los Angeles to Boston, Boston to Miami, and Miami back to Los Angeles, putting 10,000 miles on the odometer for a total gasoline cost of $140.

But the New Frontier was about to close. Within months the first OPEC oil embargo had American motorists lined up to take their turn buying suddenly-scarce and expensive gasoline. The freedom Americans had taken for granted suddenly felt confined and our prosperity under siege.

Even before that first oil embargo, the plummeting U.S. Dollar had lost one-third of its 1971 value. And with the dollar's loss of value came a loss of financial freedom and individual liberty.

The OPEC countries, wrote Greider, "were grabbing back what they had already lost – and tacking extra dollars on the price to protect themselves against future U.S. inflation."

Years later during President Jimmy Carter's Administration, gold's price soared above $850 per ounce. The biggest buyers of this gold were Muslims in oil-rich nations exchanging what they recognized as undependable dollars for the reliable value of gold.

The money they used to buy gold came from a 600 percent jump in oil prices, from $6 to more than $36 per barrel, another reflection of how the world was losing confidence in the value of the U.S. Dollar.

Beginning in 1973, and continuing to today, we Americans feel as if an OPEC drilling rig is pumping the money out of our wallets and siphoning off our nation's prosperity to foreign lands.

And for the first time in centuries, our self-sufficient nation feels threatened by the power of other nations to cut off a supply of energy on which we depend.

But OPEC's higher prices and the financial cost of the war in Southeast Asia were tiny compared to the greed of America's homegrown politicians.

## Enriching the War on Poverty

President Johnson's Great Society launched a second war, the War on Poverty. Annual welfare costs that, measured in 2008 dollars, had been $54.6 billion in 1964 began to rise like a skyrocket.

By 1981 combined state and local yearly welfare costs topped $300 billion, by 1995 $500 billion, and by 2007 these costs shot past $700 billion on a growth line that was almost vertical.

Welfare growth that liberal journalists claimed had been halted by President Ronald Reagan and then by President Bill Clinton instead has kept expanding.

Today it is the fastest growing part of government spending. Look at one visible tip of this giant, deadly iceberg that will sink America's ship of state. The number of Americans receiving Food Stamps topped 40 million in 2010, and the U.S. Department of Agriculture projects that 43 million will be on this War on Poverty program by 2011.

Former Wyoming U.S. Senator Alan Simpson, a member of President Obama's National Commission on Fiscal Responsibility and Reform, was attacked by liberals for truthfully saying that the Federal Government's biggest social program is "a milk cow with 310 million t*ts."

Projecting from government data compiled by economist Robert Rector and colleagues at the Heritage Foundation in 2009, since President Johnson's Great Society agenda became law, America's welfare state has spent approximately $17.6 trillion dollars to benefit those whom partisan politicians and bureaucrats arbitrarily define as poor.

When John F. Kennedy was president, more than half of every tax dollar went to fund national defense, a government function clearly authorized in the Constitution.

Today more than half of every tax dollar goes for "transfer payments," government policies designed to take dollars from taxpayer pockets and move those dollars into other, more politically favored pockets.

One hates to be harsh, but this represents a vast redistribution of wealth away from productive citizens and enterprises.

Much of this is rationalized as helping America win the never-ending War on Poverty – a war in which liberals have never offered the "exit strategy" and "timetable for withdrawal" they have demanded during all other wars since WWII.

## The War's General Welfare

So how is the War on Poverty progressing? As Rector and his colleagues wrote in 2009, "the military cost to the U.S. government for all military wars from the American Revolution to the present is $6.39 trillion in 2008 dollars."

With a price tag of $17.6 trillion, LBJ's ever-expanding welfare state has since 1964 cost nearly three times more than all of America's wars combined.

And the latest wars in Afghanistan and Iraq? In 2010 the Congressional Budget Office reported that President Obama's failed stimulus program far exceeded the entire cost of these wars.

America keeps fighting the War on Poverty, but poverty keeps winning.

Government policies have caused the number of people dependent on government to rise, not fall, with no end in sight. Some scholar should investigate whether tax increases to pay for the growing welfare state are pushing more Americans into poverty.

These transfer programs appear to be unconstitutional.

The U.S. Constitution says that government is to provide for the "general welfare." But as James Madison spelled out explicitly during the constitutional debates and afterwards, this should never be confused with welfare given only to selected individuals out of tax revenues.

By "general welfare" the Founders meant things that benefitted everybody in general, like a new road or town hall all could use. The Founders chose the word "general" precisely to make this clear.

Such welfare also violates the Constitution's Fifth Amendment "takings clause," according to Professor Richard Epstein of the University of Chicago Law School.

To take $100 from one citizen in order to give it to another, he argues, is in principle no different from government taking one citizen's house by eminent domain power so it can be given to another who is more politically favored.

Every tax dollar taken to fund Great Society income transfer programs should, to be constitutional, provide "fair compensation" to the taxpayer.

Therefore, argues Epstein, if you are taxed $100 to pay for your neighbor's welfare check, government should compensate you for this government "taking" with $100.

## Government Helps Itself

The apparent purpose of the Great Society was not to help the poor so much as to benefit the government and the Big Government political party.

Of every dollar spent in the War on Poverty, for many years only about 20 cents was given to the poor. Roughly 80 cents of every dollar went to provide jobs and benefits for government employees – social workers, politically-appointed welfare bosses, and others whose average salary plus benefits now add up to $120,000 per year.

If government wished to help the poor, observed Nobel-prizewinning economist Milton Friedman, it should "give them money" as directly as it could – in a check, or as a "negative income" tax credit paid to them by the Internal Revenue Service.

At the time Dr. Friedman made this point, the War on Poverty was spending the equivalent of $40,000 a year for each poor American. Simply giving each that amount would have lifted them all out of poverty.

But this, of course, was unacceptable to left-liberal politicians. It would have dismantled their huge welfare bureaucracy, reduced the size and power of government and, worse, given millions enough of a leg up to escape poverty and addictive dependence on government and Big Government politicians.

In devastated inner cities, LBJ's welfare policies have been as destructive as a military war. Young teenage girls continue to be enticed by promises of a monthly check and their own apartment provided by government if they drop out of school and become single mothers.

Many of these young women soon find themselves trapped with a baby, a limited welfare check that gets bigger each time they have another child, and little prospect for a school dropout of getting a job that pays more than a tax-free welfare check.

The liberal welfare state drove the proportion of out-of-wedlock births in inner cities above 70 percent and created generations of fatherless children for whom government assumes the role of paternalistic provider.

The Ku Klux Klan or Nazi Party could not have devised a more diabolical plan for destroying poor families. But Democratic politicians continue to expand the welfare state because its dependents vote for them.

## A Monster Unleashed

Those who follow the teachings of pioneering British economist John Maynard Keynes believe that government money given to the poor probably has a greater "multiplier" effect than President Obama's recent stimulus has had.

The poor, according to Keynesian theory, must spend money immediately to buy necessities such as food. They will rapidly spend welfare checks, and this increases the "velocity" of money in the economy, multiplying its stimulative effect by more than 1.0.

Retired Obama economic adviser Lawrence Summers predicted that the President's $814 billion Stimulus II plan would have a multiplier effect of 1.5. He was wrong. Despite almost unimaginable amounts of spending to boost growth, the U.S. economy has slowed to a snail's pace 1.7% growth, which as the *Wall Street Journal* noted dryly in September 2010 is far too slow "to restore broad-based prosperity."

Stimulus money can also speed up inflation, a loss in the purchasing power of money, as more dollars rush to the marketplace to buy an unchanged supply of goods.

Mr. Obama gave many billions of taxpayer dollars to giant banks, only to see them hold on to this cash instead of lending it to homeowners and other Americans in need of capital.

This is what Keynes called "the paradox of thrift," that the long-honored virtue of thrift and saving can harm the economy.

Back in the 1970s an unfettered government was busy printing money by the ton after Nixon severed the dollar's gold tether. This caused the value of the dollar to sink drastically and prices to rise.

Few then could see that this unleashed inflation would soon become a monster able to destroy the dollar itself, the world economy, and America as we know it.

# Chapter Two
# The Politics of Debt

*"I wish it were possible to obtain
a single amendment to our Constitution.
I would be willing to depend on that alone
for the reduction of the administration of our government
to the genuine principles of its Constitution;
I mean an additional article, taking from
the federal government the power of borrowing."*

**– Thomas Jefferson
November 26, 1789**

Behind the current economic crisis are more than four decades of cultural and political change that brought us to today's frightening crossroads.

Before we attempt to put America and our crashed dollar back together again, like Humpty Dumpty, we need to remember what has happened.

This perspective may help you reconsider some right and wrong turns America has taken along the way to where we find ourselves today.

As with the mythic Greek hero Theseus, who unwound a thread as he went in so he could find his way back out of the Minotaur's dark underground Labyrinth, this is a thread tracing how we got here that may help us find our way back to the America we once called home.

## Rancho Mirage

"From 1971 when [President Richard] Nixon abolished gold backing of the dollar, virtually all of the growth in the Western world has come from the massive increase in credit rather than from real growth of the economy," writes Egon von Greyerz, a former Swiss banker and now financial analyst for Matterhorn Asset Management AG in Zurich, Switzerland.

"The U.S. consumer price index was stable for 200 years until the early 1900s," he writes. But from 1971 to 2010 this price index "went up by almost 500%."

"The reason for this," according to von Greyerz, "is uncontrolled credit creation and money printing."

"Total U.S. debt went from $9 trillion in 1971 to $59 trillion today," he writes, "and this excludes unfunded liabilities of anywhere from $70 to $110 trillion."

During this period America's nominal Gross Domestic Product (GDP) rose from $1.1 trillion to $14.5 trillion, but this does not impress von Greyerz.

"So it has taken an increase in borrowing of $50 trillion to produce an increase in annual GDP of $13 trillion over a 40 year period," he writes.

"Without this massive increase in debt," he concludes, "the U.S. would probably have had negative growth for most of the last 39 years."

The ratio of America's debt to its Gross Domestic Product, he notes, "is now 380% and is likely to escalate substantially."

Prosperity, as those born after World War II grew up believing, was an American birthright to be taken for granted.

A century earlier the British felt this same certitude about the future well-being of their empire.

But now, as we approach the blinding light of day at the exit from the Minotaur's cave, we are beginning to see that much of our prosperity since 1971 has been a mirage, an illusion.

Like a pilot hypnotized by flying through clouds, we thought we were ascending when in fact we were falling and about to crash.

The American dream these past four decades turns out to have been obtained with a credit card whose all-consuming monstrous bill is now coming due and catching us unable to pay.

Perhaps this is what that family friend in the 1967 movie "The Graduate" meant when he told Dustin Hoffman's character that his future could center on one word: "Plastic."

Ever since President Nixon's fateful unleashing of the dollar, politicians have been printing it in huge amounts to give themselves more to spend.

Americans have had to run to keep up with the dollar's declining value. Some have barely kept pace by turning their lives into a rat race. Millions more have fallen behind.

By 2008 it took $5.31 to buy what cost $1 in 1971, when Mr. Nixon separated the dollar from its anchor in gold, according to data from University of Illinois Economics Professors Lawrence H. Officer and Samuel H. Williamson and their MeasuringWorth team of 15 university economists from American universities and Oxford University.

How many Americans today earn more than five times the income they did in 1971? This is how much more income is required – not to get ahead, but just to stay even with the relentless effects of inflation.

In purchasing power the dollar has bled away more than 81 percent of its value in far less than 40 years.

This drastic weakening of the dollar through both Republican and Democratic Administrations was often ignored by the media during these turbulent years.

This ongoing collapse of the dollar has been felt by working Americans every day as prices increase at the supermarket, the gas pump, and in almost every other part of life.

And our Middle Class, the pillar that upholds and embodies American values, has found itself dragged down with the sinking dollar.

This is why both husband and wife must work to keep their chins above an ever-rising flood tide of expenses. Back in 1950 one wage earner could support a family, just as depicted in that era's family TV shows.

In 1950 the income tax took less than three percent of an average family's income, and the rate of inflation was tiny.

Today, one in every two-earner family is working mostly to pay higher taxes, including the hidden government tax called inflation, as well as other passed-on taxes that add to the higher cost of food, fuel and every other product.

As President Reagan repeatedly said, his economists had identified at least 135 hidden taxes that increase the cost of every loaf of bread.

And when both parents must work, children come home from school to an empty house. These children are more likely to absorb their values from their peers, or from popular culture, or from public schools acting *in loco parentis*, "in place of the parents," that teach the left-liberal values of a paternalistic state.

## The Politics of Debt

President Richard Nixon is a pivotal figure in the shaping of our times. He rose to prominence as the ardent anti-Communist congressman who brought down Soviet spy Alger Hiss. (When the former Soviet Union's archives briefly opened, they confirmed that Nixon was right: Hiss had taken Soviet orders via a controller in the GRU, the Communist East German secret police.) Because of this, the left in America never ceased trying to destroy Mr. Nixon.

One paradox in our politics is that – because in our two-party system politicians run toward the center while taking their base of supporters for granted – only a liberal like John F. Kennedy could have launched a military attack against Communist Cuba or a war against Communist Vietnam, and only a bona fide anti-Communist could embrace Communist China as Nixon did.

President Nixon decided that we could drive a wedge between Maoist Red China and the Soviet Union by reaching out to China.

Trade cemented this new relationship, and today China is one of our biggest creditors and holders of our debt, enabling credit junkie America to keep feeding our addiction to spending as we turn into what authors Addison Wiggin and Kate Incontrera call I.O.U.S.A.

President Nixon placed a life-or-death long-term bet that America could turn the People's Republic of China capitalist before we transferred enough wealth to make it militarily superior to us. Thus far it appears that China has become a crony capitalist country but retained its near-totalitarian government.

One breaking point for the Soviet Union was its recognition that it could not remain in competition with Western technology without giving its brightest citizens access to computers and worldwide communications. How long can a totalitarian system survive while allowing such freedom? We shall see.

President Nixon's enemies, and his own willingness to stoop to their tactics to beat them, brought him down shortly after he won a 1972 landslide reelection against liberal Democratic Senator George McGovern.

McGovern was a decent patriot who, like Arizona conservative Senator Barry Goldwater, served as a pilot during World War II. Yet McGovern – who after leaving government and running a business said he wished he had never voted to authorize extreme business taxes and regulations – was a Progressive who helped move his party farther to the left.

In 1974 President Nixon, threatened with possible impeachment, resigned. His Vice President Gerald Ford became president and promptly pardoned his predecessor.

President Ford was a decent person, but he was an old-style rust belt Republican from Michigan whose politics might be called "Democrat Light." By compromise he would agree to pass Democratic legislation so long as it could be made a bit less onerous to business and less expensive to taxpayers.

Ford was, as Newt Gingrich once described centrist Kansas Senator Bob Dole, a "tax collector for the welfare state." He had spent so many years in politics in the minority party that, like a fish in a dark cave, he lost or never acquired the vision to see a future in which those with small government conservative views could become the ruling majority.

He famously said: "I'm a Ford, not a Lincoln."

Mr. Ford urged Americans to wear buttons that in bold letters read: WIN, Whip Inflation Now, and with good reason.

A windstorm of inflation sweeping the land had begun tearing the dollar to shreds.

By election year 1976 it cost $1.41 to purchase what cost $1 in 1971, a 41 percent increase in five years. But worse was about to come.

## Jimmy Carter's Malaise

Georgia Governor and Democrat Jimmy Carter won the presidency in 1976. He turned out lights in the White House to conserve energy, preached that America suffered malaise, and faced his own Arab oil embargo.

President Carter is proof of where a road paved with good intentions can lead. Idealism led him to cut off U.S. support for the Shah of Iran, America's strongest Persian Gulf ally, over the alleged torture of 3,000 political prisoners.

The Shah was in some ways authoritarian, but he greatly expanded rights for women, was Americanizing his Muslim nation, kept Israel supplied with oil during the Arab oil embargoes, and was key to American power projection in the Gulf. Needless to say, he was a major target for Marxist and other leftist propaganda.

Mr. Carter's withdrawal of support led to the overthrow and replacement of the Shah by radical Shiite Muslim fundamentalists – who promptly had the 3,000 prisoners, most of them agents of the godless Soviet Union, put up against a wall and shot. They also took American diplomats hostage.

This was a major triumph for radicals of many stripes, including Islamists who turned their faith into a radical political ideology bent on world conquest and creation of a global government ruled by one Muslim caliph. The toppling of the Shah gave such people hope, motivation, and a dramatic event that could persuade others to join their cause.

What soon followed was an Iran-Iraq War that killed more than 500,000 people, a war that never would have happened had the Shah remained in power. This war turned Sunni Saddam Hussein's majority-Shiite Iraq into the fourth most powerful military in the world, setting up the conflicts there that have continued to this day.

What also followed was the Soviet invasion of Afghanistan bordering Iran, another war that would never have happened with the America-backed Shah ruling Iran. Jimmy Carter's response was to wring his hands and withdraw American athletes from the Olympics in protest.

The Soviets were resisted by insurgents from throughout the Muslim world, among them an eccentric Saudi Arabian millionaire named Osama bin Laden and the warriors he funded and called Al Qaeda, "The Base." This fight persuaded bin Laden that both the Soviet Union and United States were "paper tigers" that could be bankrupted and beaten by using terrorist tactics and strategies.

What bin Laden learned in Afghanistan would be used on 9-11-2001 to kill 3,000 Americans and bring down the twin World Trade Center towers in New York City, symbols of America's might and economic potency in the world.

What bin Laden learned persuaded him that America's and the West's traditions of openness and individual liberty could be exploited to attack us.

In addition to all those who were murdered, 9-11 devastated Wall Street, costing the U.S. economy more than $1 trillion, and impeding world markets and global trade for months.

The Islamist dictatorship Mr. Carter helped install in Iran may yet unleash nuclear terrorism and war on the world that could kill many millions more and destroy world civilization.

Oddly, Mr. Carter, whose incompetence led to the deaths of more than a million people in unnecessary wars, to the oppression of tens of millions more, and to the murder of 3,000 Americans on 9-11, was later awarded the Nobel Peace Prize.

President Obama was selected the winner of this same prize by a Scandinavian socialist committee only 11 days after his inauguration, showing once again that this award now is given for ideology, not accomplishment or genuine peacemaking.

On the domestic front, inflation exploded under President Carter. Home mortgage and credit card interest rates shot into double digits. The prime lending rate topped 20%.

By election year 1980 it cost $2.03 to buy the same goods that cost only $1 in 1971.

The dollar had lost more than half its purchasing power in only nine years.

And for those with long drives to and from work in large and comfortable American cars or pickup trucks, the soaring price of gasoline bit hard into their wallets and dreams.

Gold, meanwhile, surged to $850 per Troy ounce – the same ounce that in 1971 could have been acquired by a foreign nation's bank for $35.

This was a harbinger of waning global confidence in the U.S. Dollar – and in other paper fiat currencies.

The 1971 dollar had been worth 1/35th of an ounce of gold. Nine years later it had fallen to being worth only 1/850th of an ounce of gold. Measured relative to gold's peak surge, the U.S. Dollar in less than a decade had fallen in value, at least briefly, to less than four percent of its 1971 gold value.

President Barack Obama in many ways mirrors the naivete, inexperience, weakness and indecisiveness of President Carter, and Mr. Obama is on track to cost most Americans a much, much bigger piece of their life savings than Mr. Carter did.

## The Reagan Revolution

In 1980 Americans voted overwhelmingly to replace President Carter with former California Governor Ronald Reagan. Fearful of our strong new leader, Iran released America's diplomat hostages hours before Mr. Reagan's inauguration. They had been held for 444 days.

Like European nations in today's economic crisis, Mr. Reagan chose to curtail the Carter inflation with austerity, a two year fight that led to a relatively stable dollar and many years of greater prosperity.

President Reagan cut taxes deeply, despite the House of Representatives being controlled by election-chastened Democrats. He restored optimism in the land and confidence in ideals of small government and free enterprise.

President Reagan energized the country by restoring the pride and purpose of the Founders' sense of American Exceptionalism and destiny.

Mr. Reagan's foremost goal was to defeat the Soviet Union in the Cold War. He confronted the Soviets by providing training and Stinger anti-aircraft missiles for the Muslim mujahedeen in Afghanistan and medium-range missiles to American allies in Western Europe, where green and left-wing political parties were influential in politics.

But Reagan would pay a political price, being forced to cut a deal with Democrats to expand social spending and taxes in exchange for more defense spending. Democrats promised to make other cuts in government but reneged on those promises. Government and welfare therefore grew larger under Ronald Reagan, and so did America's debt and deficit.

American power stands on two mighty legs, one military and the other economic. Our wealth was what gave Mr. Reagan victory over the Soviet Union.

When Reagan proposed building a huge anti-missile system, the Strategic Defense Initiative ridiculed as "Star Wars" by the liberal media, the chess-playing Soviet strategists saw that this would introduce uncertainty into their ability to hit American targets with ballistic missiles.

More importantly, they knew that the United States was rich enough to keep enlarging and perfecting such a system – and the Soviet planners knew that they lacked the wealth to counter this. They had been checkmated.

From a different perspective, American poker, President Reagan had raised the stakes to a level of spending they could not hope to match, so the Soviets folded. The U.S. had won, and within years the Soviet empire dissolved into the dustbin of history as its colonies pulled away.

Liberals should have loved this bloodless, non-violent warfare in which only dollars, not people, died.

President Reagan carried 49 of the 50 states in his 1984 reelection bid. He could have won 50 but chose not to campaign in Democratic nominee Walter Mondale's home state Minnesota, which Reagan lost by only a few thousand votes.

The liberal media was quick to declare that this astonishing vote of the people was not a mandate for conservatism because Mr. Reagan won with his "It's Morning in America" campaign. It of course was a strong mandate for more of the same that this charismatic leader had been doing.

The Reagan years were in many ways golden for conservatives, but the U.S. Dollar paid a steep price for political compromises, despite the President's efforts to rein in many areas of government spending.

By election year 1988 it took $2.92 to purchase goods that cost only $1 in 1971.

The dollar in 17 years had shrunk to scarcely one-third of its previous buying power, and Middle Class Americans felt the squeeze on their paychecks.

## New World Orderer

In 1988 Mr. Reagan's Vice President George H.W. Bush defeated liberal Democratic technocrat and Massachusetts Governor Michael Dukakis by a wide margin.

President Bush was a "prudent" veteran diplomat who skillfully put together a coalition to roll back Saddam Hussein's invasion of Kuwait at a low cost to the United States in money and casualties.

Mr. Bush was in some ways a Big Government conservative who advocated a "new world order" and "a kinder, gentler America," implying that his predecessor and others who shared Ronald Reagan's values were somehow neither kind nor gentle.

"Read my lips. No new taxes," he declared, then felt compelled to open those lips to swallow a tax increase from the Democratic Congress. In 1990 after victory in Kuwait his popularity in polls approached 90 percent, but he lost the 1992 election to Arkansas Governor William Jefferson Clinton in a strange and suspicious three-way race in which Clinton won only 43 percent of the popular vote.

Clinton in fact never won a majority of American votes; he won reelection in 1996 with 49 percent of the vote, but this was enough to make him the first Democratic president since Franklin Delano Roosevelt elected to two terms.

A major factor in Mr. Bush's defeat was a wobbly economy that the liberal media portrayed as worse than it actually was.

In election year 1992 it cost $3.46 to buy goods that cost $1 in 1971, and Democrats running against Bush took as their slogan "It's the Economy, Stupid."

## Clinton "Prosperity"

President Clinton ran for office vowing to cut taxes, but weeks into his presidency he called for a huge retroactive tax increase.

Centuries from now, historians may write of Mr. Clinton as a great president – a great "Republican" president who accomplished things even Ronald Reagan could not, including "ending welfare as we know it" (a Clinton welfare reform now beginning to be rolled back by the language hidden in President Obama's finance reform law), trade liberalization, and the turnover of both houses of Congress to Republican control.

Clinton was pragmatic, willing to surrender liberal principle to retain power, and a natural politician who, as Republican Mississippi Governor Haley Barbour said, "could charm the skin off a snake."

President Clinton was promiscuous, one pundit noted, not only in his personal life but also in how he governed. The first Baby Boomer president, he seemed never to have grown up or taken on adult responsibility.

Like many of today's Democratic leaders, Mr. Clinton never held a job in the private sector or met a payroll. He has worked only in government, where power is earned or stolen but money comes automatically, or in the university, where abstract utopian ideas and wordplay are often honored and rewarded above real-world achievements and integrity.

Democrats credit President Clinton with fostering prosperity during his two terms in office. They do not credit some other obvious factors.

## Republicans Take Congress

In 1994 an electorate disgusted with Democratic one-party rule in Washington, D.C., turned over both houses of Congress to the Republicans. This allowed Mr. Clinton to talk liberally for six years while firm congressional conservative hands steered American economic policy and gave people the confidence to invest.

President Clinton took office during an economic upswing that had been concealed during the 1992 campaign by a Democrat-backing liberal media.

And Mr. Clinton had ample money to spend that others had earned and set aside. This was the "Peace Dividend" from President Reagan's victory in the Cold War.

Reagan and Bush wanted American defense spending lowered gradually, both to keep the country strong and to avoid economic dislocations in places like Southern California with lots of defense industry jobs.

President Reagan would undoubtedly have preferred that this Peace Dividend go back to taxpayers to spend enriching their own families and reducing their burdens. Their sacrifices, after all, had made Cold War victory possible.

President Clinton instead dove into this pile of taxpayer money like a bear into a honey pot. He gutted America's defense budget, diverting at least $125 billion a year to spend elsewhere, and not without some liberal Republican accomplices eager to help him – and to help themselves – to the swag.

This looting of the defense and intelligence budgets is largely the source of the fabled "Clinton prosperity." He found a huge credit card that rightly belonged to others. He spent wildly and lavishly with it for things he wanted, running up the tab to then-stratospheric heights.

The other bill for Mr. Clinton's reckless slashing of America's national defense and intelligence capabilities arrived on September 11, 2001.

The dollar continued to weaken during the Clinton years, despite efforts to control spending by the Republican majority in Congress.

In election year 2000 a shopper needed $4.25 to buy what $1 could purchase in 1971. The U.S. Dollar had shriveled to only about 23 percent, less than a quarter, of its 1971 buying power.

This two-bit dollar was one reason why hard-pressed Americans were ready for a change.

## Bush Gets Gored

In 2000 the American people narrowly elected George W. Bush, despite Democratic attempts in Florida to have Democratic judges permit a selective vote recount and lawyers employed by Clinton's Vice President Al Gore using legal technicalities to throw out military absentee ballots.

Liberals should remember two things about Mr. Gore's defeat.

The first is that he could have won without Florida had he been able to carry his home state of Tennessee. Voters in that state, where people knew Gore best, strongly rejected him. So did voters in Clinton's home state of Arkansas.

The second is that Mr. Gore could easily have won the presidency in 2000 if Democrats in Congress had behaved morally and ethically.

Mr. Clinton became the first elected president ever impeached by the House of Representatives. He should then have been removed from office by the U.S. Senate, but Democrats wavered and then threw everything they could use into blocking the President's ouster.

What would have happened if the Senate removed Mr. Clinton?

Vice President Gore would have become President, and in accord with the Constitution he could have served out the less than two years remaining to Mr. Clinton and then run for two full presidential terms of his own.

In 2000, running as an incumbent president with the Clinton scandals fading in America's rear view mirror, Mr. Gore would almost certainly have been elected.

So by lacking the moral fiber to remove a tainted President Clinton, Democrats gave America eight years of President George W. Bush.

Only months after his inauguration, President Bush and the nation faced the horror of 9-11. This manmade disaster cost America not only 3,000 lives but also at least $1 Trillion in economic losses around the world.

Osama bin Laden had shown that a handful of terrorists armed only with box cutters could cause overwhelming damage to the United States.

President Bush was the grandson of a U.S. Senator and son of a president. He had the benefit of his father's advisors. He successfully prevented another shattering terrorist attack during his time in office and won reelection in 2004 by a solid margin, securing the mandate that ideological opponents said he lacked after the controversy of 2000.

President Bush responded to 9-11 with a new military doctrine of preemption, striking terrorists before they could strike us. In a world of terrorists potentially armed with nuclear or other weapons of mass destruction, we could no longer afford to wait for the certainty of a "smoking gun" if that smoke came from a mushroom cloud over New York City or Washington, D.C.

In Afghanistan Mr. Bush's forces deposed the dogmatic Taliban rulers who had given shelter, aid and comfort to bin Laden and Al Qaeda. This war even 2008 Democratic presidential candidate Barack Obama approved.

In Iraq Mr. Bush chose to play "Big Casino." Various unstable dictatorial regimes were at risk of falling in the Middle East. They could fall either towards democratic capitalist values or imitate Iran and become Islamic theocracies.

President Bush gambled that he could establish a successful, modern

Muslim democracy as an example for other Islamic nations. This would give young Muslims an alternative to Iran's theocratic dictatorship if and when the existing rulers fall from power in Saudi Arabia and other Islamic nations. It remains to be seen whether Mr. Bush's gamble will succeed or fail.

Mr. Bush, like his father, is in some ways a Big Government conservative. He promoted and signed into law a huge drug benefit, one of the largest expansions ever of the welfare state.

He is sympathetic to Latino immigrants, having grown up in Texas speaking fluent Spanish. His brother Jeb, former Governor of Florida, converted to Roman Catholicism to marry a Mexican; he, too, speaks Spanish. And in elections George W. Bush has gotten upwards of 40 percent of Mexican-American votes, an achievement Republicans may need to replicate now that Hispanics have surpassed African-Americans in numbers and become America's largest minority.

However many conservatives are offended by those who wink at violators of our immigration laws. For them, the news footage of President Bush riding in a Border Patrol dune buggy near Yuma, Arizona, was reminiscent of liberal Michael Dukakis playing soldier in an Army tank.

In November 2008 voters rejected the Republican presidential nominee who shared Mr. Bush's view of immigration, Arizona Senator John McCain, in favor of a fledgling lawmaker from Illinois, Senator Barack Obama.

In 2008 the dollar was now worth less than 19 cents of its 1971 value and was still going down.

The dollar's continuing downward spiral was, by election time, only one factor in much larger economic, political and social crises that its drop helped cause.

# A Financial 9-11

Less than two months before the 2008 election, fear of a global economic meltdown pressured President Bush into signing a bill to stop the collapse of major banks and other institutions.

This economic shock at first looked like a financial 9-11, a bolt out of the blue that had taken the world by surprise.

Some analysts, however, had watched these forces converging for a long time and had warned investors to take shelter.

When a doomsday rock, a flying mountain of an asteroid, is about to crash into Earth, where can you find shelter from its devastation? Before this book ends, you will know where and how to escape what is coming.

Having looked at the politics leading to the current Great Recession, we next need to focus on other converging forces behind this crisis that most do not yet see or fully understand.

# Part Two
# Dream House

# Chapter Three
# Houses of Cards

*"We have had, for the last quarter century,*
*a continuing lie....*
*We tried to have houses without savings.*
*We tried to have government without responsibility.*
*You can't do it."*

- Newt Gingrich
former Speaker of the
House of Representatives
February 20, 2010

The economic devastation of today's Great Recession is immense. The shock wave of this bubble bursting circled the world in 2008 and 2009, wiping out $50 trillion in investor equity – equal to nearly one year's Gross Domestic Product of the entire planet. At least $10 trillion of that loss was from American equities, as a stock market that had topped 14,000 plummeted to 6,600.

The average home price in America has fallen by about 30 percent or more, a loss to homeowners of more than $5 trillion in what for most was the biggest investment in their lives, the equity nest egg many had planned to use for retirement or their children's college education.

The Great Unraveling has cost more than five million people their homes, lost to foreclosure or fire sales. Millions more have lost their life savings, spent to hang on in what Federal Reserve Chair Ben Bernanke called an "unusually uncertain" wild roller coaster economy.

With roughly one third of the U.S. economy connected in some way to housing and home values, the ripple effect of this real estate price plunge continues to be felt in fewer sales and more job layoffs in businesses ranging from homebuilding to appliance manufacture, from cable television to garden supply.

Few believe this crisis is near its end. Many fear that worse, perhaps much worse, is soon to come. We may be only one bad newspaper headline from even steeper drops in home prices and the stock market – or even a global economic collapse.

And 65 percent of us, according to a September 2010 NBC/Wall Street Journal poll, now fear that America has gone into decline – and that our children could enjoy less prosperity, opportunity and freedom than we have known.

How did this happen? Who is responsible? And what is likely to come next?

The liberal media tells us that greedy capitalist "banksters" are the cause of today's crisis. Giant banks certainly share a portion of the blame, but there is lots to go around.

Homeowners who walked away from their "underwater" house and mortgage hurt not only the lenders who trusted them, but also their former neighbors whose property values fell as a result of these unethical "strategic defaults" next door.

The biggest villain in today's drama is the liberal media's ally, the very government that liberal journalists tell us should be given vastly more power to fix a problem that politicians and their policies caused.

## Carter's Poison Pill

Like so much that now threatens and bedevils the United States, the seeds of today's Great Recession were planted by President Jimmy Carter, who came to power because of the political and gold-abandoning economic problems that brought down President Richard Nixon.

In 1977 Mr. Carter signed into law the Community Reinvestment Act (CRA). Originally sold as only a law to gather data on bank lending to minorities, CRA immediately became a hammer whose data was used to accuse banks of racism and discrimination in their lending policies.

The liberal media accused banks of "redlining," making few loans in certain neighborhoods. The media almost never mentioned that the Federal Housing Administration (FHA) began imposing "redlining" during the 1930s, mapping and discouraging loans in deteriorating neighborhoods where property values were declining, and that most banks had been pushed to adopt this government guideline.

Making loans on the basis of politicized social engineering rather than credit worthiness is never a sound business decision.

And those who took out what came to be called "liar loans" – in which buyers, not required to provide documentation, simply claimed to make far more income than was true – have more responsibility for what has happened than do the government-coerced banks.

If the government were scrupulous about financial propriety and law, it would now be checking whether borrowers committed fraud by making false income claims. What does it tell us that left-liberal politicians are not lifting a finger to do this?

## Strong-arming the Banks

By the late 1970s the CRA was already being used by both government and radical activists to intimidate banks into lowering their lending standards so that more poor and minority borrowers could qualify for loans.

In 1993 new President Bill Clinton, backed by a Democrat-dominated Congress, greatly expanded this power. Banks were now given a so-called "CRA rating" of their minority lending policies and practices, a measure that involved any of four government bureaucracies.

Contrary to recent liberal propaganda, banks are not "under-regulated." They have long been among the most heavily regulated institutions in America, and with such often-arbitrary government rules come strings and political interference.

Banks given a "poor" CRA rating could be refused permission to expand as their competitors did, or to add new branches.

"Banks that got poor reviews were punished," wrote University of Texas economics Professor Stan Liebowitz. "Some saw their merger plans frustrated; others faced direct legal challenges by the Justice Department."

"The pressure to comply with CRA was astounding," recalled former bank manager Noel Sheppard, "especially at Great Western as it was expanding throughout the country. Its ability to acquire other institutions was directly related to its CRA rating."

"When legislation was pending in 1999 during the Clinton Administration to permit banks to diversify into selling investment securities," writes economist Thomas Sowell of Stanford University's Hoover Institution in his 2009 book *The Housing Boom and Bust*, "the White House urged 'that banks given unsatisfactory ratings under the 1977 Community Reinvestment Act be prohibited from enjoying the new diversification privileges' of this legislation."

Either implicitly or explicitly, banks were expected to meet an arbitrary quota for loans to poor and racial minority borrowers to get a CRA rating. At the high point of this policy, one key mortgage institution was directed to have 55 percent of its mortgages helping these minorities.

## Ninja Loans

What followed, wrote *Investor's Business Daily's* Terry Jones in 2008, was that "in the name of diversity, banks began making huge numbers of loans that they previously would not have. They opened branches in poor areas to lift their CRA ratings...."

A large percentage of these were what the bankers nicknamed "Ninja" loans, given mostly to minority applicants who had No Income, No Job, and No Assets.

In 2010 former Republican Speaker of the House Newt Gingrich described what the Clinton Administration strong-armed bankers into offering:

"If you can't afford to buy a house, we'll waive your credit. If you can't afford to buy a house, we'll let you come in without a down payment. If you can't afford to buy a house, we'll let you have three years without paying any principal. If you can't afford to buy a house, we'll give it to you below interest rate. And guess what: None of it worked."

"That's how the contagion began," wrote Jones. "With those changes, the sub-prime market took off. From a mere $35 billion in loans in 1994, it soared to $1 trillion by 2008."

Behind the Clinton Administration policies of housing for the poor was a radical leftist ideal of equality that it was not enough to provide shelter for the poor. The unfortunate poor, Mr. Clinton believed, should be given housing as good as that owned by the rich, the "winners of life's lottery."

In the name of radical equality, for example, the Clinton Administration used taxpayer money to give poor people homes in San Diego's wealthiest beachfront California Riviera suburb La Jolla (Spanish for "The Jewel"), a community as pricey as Beverly Hills or the movie star beach colony at Malibu.

As part of its new left-liberal vision of "mixed-income communities" that include the poor, the Clinton Administration also established halfway houses for felons and drug addicts in homes in such well-to-do neighborhoods, thereby endangering and driving down the property values of those next door who had worked hard to earn their dream homes in what until then had been safe upscale communities.

## Fannie and Freddie

To enable this ideology of the redistribution of property wealth to the poor, a Democrat-controlled Congress gave two nominally-private for-profit banks approval to backstop risky bank lending to poor people who, prior to CRA, would never have qualified for a mortgage.

These two banks were empowered by law, wrote Jones, "to finance it all by buying loans from banks, then repackaging and securitizing them for resale on the open market....

"Wall Street eagerly sold the new mortgage-backed securities. Not only were they pooled investments, mixing good and bad, but they were backed with the implicit guarantee of government."

These two banks quickly "grew to become monsters, accounting for nearly half of all U.S. mortgage loans," reported *Investor's Business Daily* in September 2008. "At the time of their bailouts this month, they held $5.4 trillion in loans on their books. About $1.4 trillion of those were sub-prime."

These two "monsters" that today hold an even larger percentage of U.S. mortgages are the Federal National Mortgage Association (FNMA), popularly known as Fannie Mae, and the Federal Home Loan Mortgage Corporation (FHLMC), known as Freddie Mac.

Both are GSEs, government-sponsored enterprises, that although nominally "private" (like the U.S. Post Office or Federal Reserve Board) are deeply intertwined with the government and are backed by government resources.

Fannie Mae was founded in 1938, during the Great Depression, to acquire the loans of other banks and thereby free them to make new local loans. It would then "securitize" these mortgages by bundling them into securities for sale.

What we now call Fannie Mae is the private stockholder-owned corporation created by Congress in 1968 when it spun off half the original entity, apparently to remove Fannie Mae's activity from the federal budget.

Freddie Mac was created in 1970. Like Fannie Mae, it pools, securitizes and sells mortgages (a word from the Old French that means a "vow onto death").

## Piggy Banking

The relationship between Fannie Mae & Freddie Mac, the government, and the Democratic Party, has been more than intertwined; it has been incestuous.

*Investor's Business Daily* describes Fannie Mae and Freddie Mac as a "Democrat Piggy Bank."

Between 1989 and 2008 Democratic Senator Chris Dodd, Democrat of Connecticut and Chairman of the powerful Senate Committee on Banking, Housing and Urban Affairs, pocketed at least $164,900 in campaign contributions from Fannie Mae and Freddie Mac employees and Fannie-Freddie Political Action Committees.

Senator John Kerry, Democrat of Massachusetts and his party's 2004 presidential nominee, received at least $111,000 from Fannie & Freddie. Senator Hillary Clinton, Democrat of New York, fattened her coffers with at least $75,550. Rep. Barney Frank, Democrat of Massachusetts, took more than $40,000.

One of the top two beneficiaries of such Fannie Mae-Freddie Mac political contributions was then-Senator Barack Obama, Democrat of Illinois, who during only two years of service in Congress larded his campaign war chest with at least $120,349 from these mortgage monsters.

Republican lawmakers also received contributions from Fannie & Freddie, although usually in smaller amounts. Most beneficiaries from both parties held seats on committees that could influence these entities.

Senator Dodd and Congressman Frank chaired committees with regulatory authority over Fannie Mae and Freddie Mac, yet took their money with no concern that this could be seen as a conflict of interest, or even a bribe or kickback.

## Political Profiteers

These quasi-public entities have also been used to pour other easy cash into prominent Democrat pockets. Rahm Emanuel, President Obama's White House Chief of Staff until October 2010, was appointed to the board of Freddie Mac by a departing President Clinton in 2000. Emanuel was paid at least $320,000 for the onerous work of attending six board meetings per year on this patronage job.

When scandals arose concerning campaign contributions and accounting irregularities involving Freddie Mac during Emanuel's tenure as a director there, the Clinton Administration stonewalled Freedom of Information Act requests for Freddie Mac documents that might have incriminated Emanuel.

Emanuel resigned from Freddie Mac's board in 2001 to run for Congress. During his brief time as an Illinois Congressman, Emanuel also pocketed more than $51,000 in Fannie & Freddie campaign contributions.

Emanuel is famous for spelling out the chief political tactic of the Obama Administration: "You never want a serious crisis to go to waste. What I mean by that is that it's an opportunity to do things you could not do before."

However the money Emanuel received from Freddie Mac is small compared to how other Democrat political profiteers have done with Fannie & Freddie. Jamie Gorelick, President Clinton's Deputy Attorney General, was appointed Vice Chair of Freddie Mac and earned a reported $26 million.

Longtime Democratic insider James Johnson was CEO of Freddie Mac for seven years before serving as head of Senator Obama's Vice-Presidential selection committee. He got a reported $21 million from Freddie Mac.

Franklin Delano Raines was Assistant Director of President Carter's Domestic Policy Staff from 1977 until 1979. In 1996 he retired as Fannie Mae's Vice Chairman to become President Clinton's Director of the U.S. Office of Management and Budget. In 1999 he returned to Fannie Mae as its CEO, where he resumed his influence on its controversial lending policies.

Raines reportedly walked away from Fannie Mae with $90 million in salary and bonuses he had maximized by, among other things, pushing this entity to take on large numbers of what proved to be risky loans.

Raines and Johnson both denied that they were "members of Mr. Obama's political circle" as a *Washington Post* editorial claimed. Raines insisted that he had merely "gotten a couple of calls" from the Obama campaign and had given it advice on "general housing, economic issues."

## The Spending Continues

In September 2008 both Fannie & Freddie were placed under the conservatorship of the Federal Housing Finance Agency (FHFA). Both continue to function.

Rep. Barney Frank, Chairman of the House Financial Services Committee, in a 2010 interview on CNBC described the two mortgage giants as a "public policy instrument....a kind of public utility."

While private banks were attacked for paying bonuses to their executives, Fannie & Freddie got little heat in 2009 for their million-dollar retention bonuses for their top executives.

On Christmas Eve 2009, the U.S. Treasury announced a "taxpayer massacre lifting the $400 billion cap on potential losses for Fannie Mae and Freddie Mac as well as the limits on what the failed companies can borrow," reported the *Wall Street Journal*. "The Treasury is hoping no one notices...."

In 2010 the Obama Administration announced that it was bailing out Fannie & Freddie to the tune of about $150 billion. But these entities continue to acquire toxic assets from other banks, and to bleed red ink that taxpayers will soon be bled to replace. Fannie & Freddie have, in effect, been given unlimited spending authority to absorb toxic debts.

Although President Obama signed into law a new 2,300 page bill to regulate American financial institutions, that bill contained NO NEW REGULATIONS over Fannie Mae or Freddie Mac, entities that played a huge role in bringing on the current Great Recession. So much for "change we can believe in."

Ironically, one entity eliminated by the new financial reform law is the Office of Thrift Supervision, which had played a role in supervising Fannie & Freddie after the current crisis began.

It seems grimly funny that the government office charged with overseeing thrift(s) is the one axed by President Obama.

Believe it or not, a new government program called Affordable Advantage in four states – Idaho, Massachusetts, Minnesota and Wisconsin – is providing mortgages to poor people with no money down.

State agencies in this program, as the *New York Times* reported in September 2010, "buy the loans from lenders, then sell them as securities to Fannie Mae. Because the government now owns 80 percent of Fannie Mae, taxpayers are on the hook if the loans go bad."

With no structural changes to these GSEs, we can expect more taxpayer losses.

## ACORN Harvest

Democrats have other ways to benefit from the CRA housing policies launched by President Carter and massively enlarged by President Clinton. These policies have become, both directly and indirectly, a rich source of seed money for radical community activists, including young Barack Obama.

Such activists have become the shock troops of the Democratic Party, especially in inner cities. They propagandize poor residents with messages of class warfare, register them to vote (sometimes packing voter rolls with ghost voters as well), and get people to fill out absentee ballots or transport them to the polling place on election day.

The best known of such groups is ACORN, the Association of Community Organizations for Reform Now.

Founded in 1970 by two 1960s New Left activist veterans of Students for a Democratic Society (SDS), ACORN has pursued several agendas, the two biggest being voter registration and housing rights.

While a community organizer in Chicago, Barack Obama held seminars to teach radical techniques to ACORN leaders. Mr. Obama also was one of several lawyers representing ACORN in a motor-voter legal case. For nearly two years Mr. Obama was Illinois head of a voter registration organization that was one of almost 100 groups run by ACORN.

Over the years left-liberal local, state and federal politicians and bureaucrats have funneled taxpayer money to ACORN and its many organizations.

When Bill Clinton was near the end of his presidency, the Department of Housing and Urban Development estimated, ACORN in the 2000 budget year received $42 million taxpayer dollars.

Congress's House Oversight and Government Reform Committee estimated that between 1994 and 2009 ACORN received at least $53 million in taxpayer dollars.

## ACORN Shakedowns

Both sides of the aisle in Congress became familiar with ACORN. In 1991 the radical group staged a two-day takeover of the House Banking Committee hearing room to protest attempts to weaken President Carter's CRA, which had already become the most powerful leftist tool for transferring private property to the poor.

Adept in the confrontation tactics of Chicago radical Saul Alinsky – the same community organizer Hillary Clinton wrote her college thesis to honor – ACORN was quick to smear or demean any who stood in the way of what its leaders wanted.

Banking giants "Chase Manhattan and J.P. Morgan donated hundreds of thousands of dollars to ACORN," according to an investigation by Michelle Minton of the Competitive Enterprise Institute, "at about the same time they were to apply for permission to merge and needed to comply with CRA regulations."

Fannie Mae and Freddie Mac donated funds to ACORN and its organizations. These entities also bought bank mortgages of Ninja borrowers if those borrowers had paid to take "mortgage counseling," and ACORN pocketed that loot squeezed from poor borrowers by becoming one of the nation's biggest mortgage counselors.

After his election, President Barack Obama talked for a time as if, despite allegations that ACORN was guilty of widespread voter registration fraud, he would give this radical organization a major role in the 2010 U.S. Census and channel up to $8 billion of taxpayer money into ACORN coffers.

This sparked loud objections because a dishonest Census count could be used to put more congressional districts in Democrat-dominated places and fewer in Republican-majority places, thereby tilting reapportionment leftward and rigging future congresses by giving an unfair advantage to Democrats.

ACORN soon became too much of a pariah for President Obama to bankroll. Among the factors discrediting the leftist organization were secretly-made videotapes of ACORN office employees offering ways to break various laws.

The brother of ACORN's founder was caught embezzling almost a million dollars from the organization's tax-exempt coffers.

But perhaps the final nail in ACORN's coffin was its firing of employees who tried to unionize. These employees testified that ACORN bosses expected them to work 54 hours per week for a yearly salary of $22,000. ACORN sought, but failed to get, an exemption from minimum wage laws. This left-wing organization was recruiting the poor and, despite its sizable cash flow, was keeping these workers poor.

## "Tear Them Down"

Capitalism defeated Communism in the marketplace of the real world for many reasons. One was that a socialist command economy run by a few government planners lacks the sophisticated natural feedback mechanisms of a free marketplace. Without such information, socialist bosses make foolish decisions.

This happens whenever government planners decide that they are smarter than the free market and try to impose their will.

This is what has happened with President Obama and his liberal predecessors trying to command American banking and housing.

And compounding their errors have been left-liberal ideology and partisan opportunism.

In the name of social equality, Presidents Carter, Clinton and Obama have showered privilege and favoritism on groups that just happen to vote overwhelmingly for Democratic candidates and in other ways advance the agenda of the Democratic Party.

To a man with a hammer, every problem looks like a nail.

To the worshipper of Big Government like Barack Obama, the only solution he sees to every problem is more taxes, more regulation, and more power in the hands of government.

The logical corollary to this in Mr. Obama's ideology is that nothing is acceptable that makes government smaller or weaker (unless it only shrinks and weakens the U.S. military). This explains his unwillingness even to consider free market solutions to today's problems.

"The administration made a bet that a rising economy would solve the housing problem and now they are out of chips," a former Clinton Administration housing official Howard Glaser told the *New York Times*. "They are deeply worried and don't really know what to do."

What President Obama has turned to is the example of other past and present left-liberals such as President Franklin Delano Roosevelt.

During the Great Depression FDR's solution for poor farmers was a mix of policies that included price supports, subsidies for not growing crops, and the deliberate destruction of excess food supply.

In a world with starving people, millions of gallons of milk were poured down drains so that the milk that remained would fetch higher prices for farmers.

If this seems crazy, then consider what today's left-liberals are contemplating and already doing.

Douglas Duncan, the vice president and chief economist for Fannie Mae, in 2010 proposed that the problem with American home prices is that too big a supply of homes for sale exists, along with a "shadow inventory" of foreclosed homes owned by banks.

Duncan's solution in a chilled economy where many are homeless: "Some of that shadow inventory could have to be torn down," the *Washington Post* quotes him as saying.

"It's un-American to think about tearing down housing," Duncan told a Texas gathering of journalists. "But we have a long history of ghost towns."

Yes, the ghosts of what we left behind continue to haunt today's crisis.

The City of Detroit is making plans to bulldoze some of its housing as a way of making what remains more valuable and neighborhoods more livable.

Meanwhile, liberals find ways to feed the vultures of the Great Unraveling. During the crisis savvy contractors from around the country have been snapping up abandoned homes in Detroit for anywhere from $1 to $2,500. They then turn to the government and offer to rent these homes to the poor.

The government obliges, taking over responsibility for each home while paying the contractors at least $700 per month out of taxpayer money. In less than four months the contractor owns the property, owes virtually nothing in property taxes because of each house's low purchase price, and thereafter pockets at least $8,400 per year as pure gravy from houses bought for as little as $1.

It helps, of course, to be a favored government insider seeking such opportunities. But in cases like Detroit's, one new idea of "entrepreneurship" in America consists of finding and milking government programs at taxpayer expense.

This is the brave new world that community organizers such as Barack Obama created, a bleak and bankrupt urban rustbelt wasteland in which the government-privileged few pick the pockets of the many working taxpayers.

## "Let It Collapse"

Outside of today's ruling elite and their circle of media comrades, saner voices can yet be heard.

"Housing needs to go back to reasonable levels," says Anthony B. Sanders, a real estate finance professor at George Mason University. "If we keep trying to stimulate the market, that's the definition of insanity."

The problem with housing, many free market economists now say, is that President Obama's ill-conceived stimulus and other rescue efforts never let the "housing bubble" fully deflate.

Mr. Obama is spending hundreds of billions of taxpayer dollars to prop up an artificial situation that sooner or later will collapse.

Government caused today's problems by giving incentives for people to sink their savings into homes by making mortgage interest and local property taxes deductible from Federal taxes.

Government and the Federal Reserve Board then put the value of those homes on a roller coaster of easy money and artificial low interest rates while at the same time strong-arming banks into giving millions of mortgages to ninjas who were unlikely ever to pay back these loans.

Even the *New York Times* by September 2010 was quoting economists who say "Let it collapse."

"We have had enough artificial support and need to let the free market do its thing," housing analyst Ivy Zelman told the New York Times.

The message from such experts is clear: let the free market determine true house values, even if these are 10 to 40 percent lower than today's reduced prices.

Let the free market end today's economic uncertainties by pulling away the government props so homes can be purchased by people who have earned the right to own them.

Likewise, a day is fast approaching when even the liberal *New York Times* will say of America's then-hyperinflated dollar: "Let it collapse. The old dollar died heroically, paying off the crazy, impossible debts we all ran up. Let us bury the dollar with honor and embrace a new, more honest currency."

Before we look that deeply into the Obamanomics rabbit hole, we need to understand the human side of today's immediate crisis in housing and the American economy.

# Chapter Four
# Betting the House

*"The strength of a nation
derives from the integrity of the home."*

**– Confucius**

Recent liberal housing policies are the biggest cause of today's Great Recession and of the financial nightmare of millions of homeowners.

Yet the roots of today's Great Recession also reach farther back – to President Nixon's final break of the U.S. Dollar's link to gold, and even to 1913, the same year the Federal Reserve Board and Income Tax began.

In 1913 the U.S. Government offered a rare compensation to citizens for its newborn Fed seizing control of America's money supply and the government imposing an income tax.

The government made interest on loans tax-deductible at the federal level. This deductibility applied to home mortgages as well as other loans, including those that had nothing to do with business.

Until 1986 Americans could deduct the interest run up on their credit cards from their income tax. Government repealed this, but it kept the mortgage interest deduction in place.

People also could sell a house and owe no capital gains tax on their profit so long as they within two years rolled that profit into the purchase of another home.

This tax law made buying a home on time possible for many who otherwise could not afford it. Its rollover provision made homes a good way to save money.

In a pre-CRA era, buying a home was a serious decision. A buyer seeking a mortgage had to have excellent credit, a proven income, and typically the savings to pony up 20 percent of the home's cost as a down payment.

These rules gave great stability to the housing market. Banks knew that the borrower was a good credit risk. The down payment invested the buyer in a home, making it costly to walk away. Those who stopped making monthly payments would lose the house, including their equity paid into it. The down payment also minimized bank concerns that the house might lose value.

In Canada these tried-and-true old rules still largely apply today. And Canada – surprise, surprise – has not plunged into a housing or a banking crisis, except insofar as our huge economic problems have spilled across the Canadian border to affect their income and unemployment rate.

American mortgage interest tax deductibility did nudge millions of people into buying rather than renting their homes.

This was widely seen as positive. Homeowners tended to be more involved with their communities, in part because of a desire that their property taxes be spent wisely and that public schools remain good. Home ownership was a key to the "Father Knows Best" values of family, faith, friendly neighbors, social cohesion and rootedness.

And governments benefitted not only from property taxes but also from citizens holding the bulk of their wealth in a form that could not easily be put in a suitcase and carried out of the country beyond the grasp of American tax collectors. Homeowners who stopped paying property tax would find their homes seized by the local government landlord.

## Leave It to Beaver

The "Father Knows Best" world of the 1950s was in many ways astonishingly different from that of today's young people.

In, say, 1954 a typical family paid two percent of what it earned as income tax. The average income was $3,960. A large new car cost $1,700. A new home cost $10,250 and was viewed as a secure, stable investment, not a way to get rich in a hurry.

The U.S. Dollar was tied to gold, which had a steady value of $35 per ounce. Inflation during the 1950s was typical of what happens with a gold-backed currency. What cost $1 in 1950 cost only $1.15 in 1960.

Even during the volatile 1960s, with Presidents Johnson and Nixon printing money to fund American forces in Southeast Asia, the gold-backed dollar helped keep inflation in check.

In 1970, just prior to Mr. Nixon's abandonment of the Bretton Woods Agreement link between the dollar and gold, it cost consumers only $1.31 to buy what they could have purchased for one dollar in 1960; this measure of inflation during the 1960s grew by only three percent per year during these years of social change.

This meant that, as in "Leave It to Beaver," a family could live comfortably with one wage earner. Typically women could choose to stay home and be with their children. Few children were "latchkey kids" who came home from school to an empty house with little adult supervision.

By 2009 much had changed. In the typical family both husband and wife now held jobs, with the lower income earner working mostly to pay the family's taxes and to offset rising prices.

Ever since, we have lived in a nation where in the average family both parents are away all workday and their children do become "latchkey kids." The bonds of family values are weakened. Children are raised less by their parents and more by peers and teachers in government schools, whose values become more influential.

The weakening dollar caused much of this underlying inflation, but it was masked by several factors. Feminism, for example, persuaded many women that going to work asserted their rights and abilities and made them the equal of wage-earning men.

This both masked and caused inflation, because the higher family income brought more dollars to the supermarket to buy the same supply of potatoes – and thus the law of supply and demand simply drove up prices. It took more dollars to buy those potatoes. The two-income family soon found that rising prices left them no better off – but they were now trapped with prices that required two incomes instead of the one that during the 1950s was enough.

In 2009 the average income was $44,000, but bouts of inflation since President Nixon broke the dollar's gold anchor meant that a shopper now needed $7.98 to buy what cost only $1 in 1954.

In 2009 an ordinary new car cost $28,400. The average new home nationwide cost $210,000.

And in 2009 taxes bit hard on middle-class wallets. In California a typical resident could lose 20 percent or more of income to federal income taxes, several percent more in state income tax and to a sales tax of about 8.75 percent on almost everything purchased.

California cities, in violation of Proposition 13's limit on direct property taxes, typically charge property-related homeowner fees such as street "tree-trimming" charges that used to be covered by the property tax; this appears to be part of a long-term government approach to pocket the old taxes, then gradually find ways to charge taxpayers a second time with separate fees for each government service. And on top of this come a bevy of hidden taxes that raised the price of everything.

By one estimate, 37 percent of the cost of a new home in California comes from hidden government taxes and regulations. It is not free, for example, when a community restricts land use because of environmental concerns. This can make every new house smaller in size and much larger in price.

Older Americans grew up thinking of America as a country that cherishes free enterprise. Truth be told, our country has the second heaviest business taxes of any advanced industrial nation in the world. Only Japan taxes business more.

Ironically, from a business point of view even Russia and Communist China are now less taxing and regulation-crazy than the U.S. These factors have caused companies to move literally millions of jobs offshore.

The annual Heritage Foundation/Wall Street Journal assessment of global economic freedom has in recent years dropped the U.S. down to only the eighth freest economy and now defines us as "mostly free."

By 2009 American families may have had a big-screen TV, ipods, cell phones and other technological advances. But in many ways we are poorer than we were in 1954.

## The Cost of Giving Up Gold

Here is something to contemplate. To buy the average $10,250 house in 1954 cost, in gold worth $35 to the ounce, 293 ounces of gold or 2.6 years of income.

In 2009 the average new $210,000 home cost 221 ounces of gold or 4.7 years of income.

In other words, in 2009 it took 80 percent more years of labor to buy a house.

It took 25 percent LESS gold, because gold by 2009 had risen to $950 per ounce.

Suppose that back in 1954 you had purchased 293 ounces of gold for $10,250. In 2009 that gold would have been worth $278,214.28.

(And in 2010, with gold around or above $1,300 per ounce, this golden investment would have risen to $380,900, while home prices fell.)

Let's stay with 2009, the last year for which we have final numbers. Subtract the 1954 house cost from $278,214.28 and this leaves $267,964.28 as a profit.

Gold's rising value in dollars would be equivalent to earning interest of $4,872.07 per year for 55 years, nearly 50 percent per year, on your original $10,250 investment in gold. Imagine how big this would be with the magic of compound interest.

With your 2009 gold profit you could buy a new home today for $210,000 and have $57,964.28 left in your pocket. And gold has gotten almost one-third more valuable since 2009 while houses since 2005 have lost a third or more of their value.

This, in effect, is what President Nixon cost America when he severed the dollar's anchor, destroying a U.S. Dollar that was literally as good as gold.

Vladimir Lenin, founder of the Communist Soviet Union, said that the way to destroy the capitalist bourgeoisie was to "grind them down between the wheels of taxation and inflation."

This is precisely what liberal presidents since Richard Nixon have done.

In 1933 an earlier left-liberal Democrat, President Franklin Delano Roosevelt, made it illegal for Americans to own gold bullion, and that law was still in effect in 1954. One would have had to secure gold in the form of numismatic coins, which were never confiscated under FDR's Executive Order.

However, in 1975 the ban on gold ownership was lifted, so people cannot say that they have had no way to protect themselves by creating their own personal gold standard.

## Liberals Rob the Middle Class

The aim of left-liberals and so-called Progressives, with the 1913 establishment of the Federal Reserve Board and the income tax – and continuing today – apparently has been to create disintegrating paper money....all the better to tax you with.

Economic historian G. Edward Griffin explains this provocative idea in his history of the Federal Reserve Board *The Creature from Jekyll Island.*

"Inflation has now been institutionalized at a fairly constant 5% per year. This has been determined to be the optimum level for generating the most revenue without causing public alarm. A 5% devaluation applies, not only to the money earned this year, but to all that is left over from previous years. At the end of the first year, a dollar is worth 95 cents. At the end of the second year, the 95 cents is reduced again by 5%, leaving its worth at 90 cents, and so on. By the time a person has worked 20 years, the government will have confiscated 64% of every dollar he saved over those years. By the time he has worked 45 years, the hidden tax will be 90%. The government will take virtually everything a person saves over a lifetime."

Our Nixonian no-longer-gold-anchored paper dollar is losing value every decade to inflation, and this is happening not by accident but by design to those who keep their savings in politician paper promissory fiat dollars.

Government tax and regulatory policies are snatching away our earnings, in part by making almost everything we buy more expensive.

Because of this, the American working class in 2010 has scarcely increased its real purchasing power in almost 40 years.

And this grand paper dollar con game uses other tools as well. Liberals and progressives prey on human envy and covetousness. "Let's tax the rich who have more than you do," they say.

By such manipulation they persuaded people to accept the so-called "progressive" income tax, the Alternative Minimum Tax (AMT), and, probably, after this coming election a heavier tax "on those earning more than $250,000 per year."

This and a thousand other penalties and surcharges have been sold as targeting "only the rich." And thus today the successful Middle Class American, whose dollar income (but not purchasing power) has risen mostly because of inflation, now pays a confiscatory tax rate that was originally supposed to rob only the rich.

Large parts of President Obama's new laws include tax and fee increases that are NOT indexed for inflation. Do you really believe this is accidental?

The coming hyperinflation will soon make you "rich," just as the AMT has for millions of middle class Americans, and subject you to these government money grabs.

## Feeling Rich

By 2005 the median sales price of a single-family home had risen in less than a decade by 79 percent in New York, by 110 percent in Los Angeles, and by 127 percent in San Diego.

Americans briefly felt wealthy as, in places such as Los Angeles, the price of an average decent suburban home approached $1 million.

America briefly may have had new millions of "millionaires," at least on paper.

The trouble was that we never had enough buyers with a million dollars apiece to buy all those homes.

Those soaring real estate prices got so high so fast that people found themselves luckily owning homes that at their income they could no longer afford to buy.

Many parents in Southern California felt the strange anguish of seeing their adult children move away because young married couples eager to start a family of their own could not afford even a small "starter" house in the communities where they grew up.

People thought that they had become wealthy by a rising tide that lifted all property prices. But when they looked down, they saw that they were high atop an unstable gigantic price wave that was about to crash into the rocky shore of reality.

What will happen when people wake up and realize that - in infla-tion-adjusted dollars - they are earning no more today than they did three decades ago?

For most, the stagnant wages of the Middle Class have remained masked by inflation, the feminism-driven shift to two-income families, and the brief feeling of wealth that came not from earnings but from borrowing against short-lived high home values.

The collapse in home prices is now dragging many from being Middle Class to working poor. People are starting to ask if America can afford a government as big as the one President Obama is creating.

## Castles in the Air

Sometime around 2005-2006 a mass hypnotic spell began to break, and when it did the vast bubble of stratospheric property prices popped.

Real estate prices simply could rise no higher into the unbreathable thin air where only the wealthy could afford to buy homes.

As in 1929, or the 17th Century Dutch tulip mania, people had been paying sky-high prices on margin, mortgage money borrowed with little or nothing down, betting that prices would keep rising, pay off these debts, and make them winners.

Cable television channels such as HGTV launched programs encour-aging people to "flip" homes – to buy them with small down payments, then after a few months of cosmetic improvement to resell them for tens or hundreds of thousands more.

This was a get-rich-quick scheme, one of many that flourished across the country, that promised wealth without much work. For those who grew up in a consumer culture and political culture whose propa-ganda told them wealth was their birthright, this was a seductive come-on they were all too eager to embrace.

Millions were playing musical chairs, expecting to unload their risk

onto the next home buyer and pocket huge profits from this speculation. But when the music suddenly stopped, many were caught holding
heavily-mortgaged homes they could neither afford to keep nor profit-
ably sell.

Awakening from this mass delusion of wealth was chilling, because
many had believed it and spent money as if they were millionaires.

## Lending Frenzy

While housing prices skyrocketed until around 2006, televisions
were full of ads urging people to take out home equity loans. "You can
borrow up to 125 percent of your home's appraised value," the message
went. "You can borrow without documenting your income."

"In the 2004-2006 period," writes former president of the Federal
Reserve Bank of Cleveland Jerry L. Jordan, "MEWs (mortgage equity
withdrawals) reached 9% of disposable income, which....fueled an
extraordinary boom in auto sales, furnishings, appliances, consumer
imports of all kinds, as well as remittances to other countries."

Remittances?  Lending standards for mortgages became so loose that
experts estimate as many as five million illegal aliens may have joined
the throngs receiving home loans. Banks and the government, of course,
refuse to release such information and thereby make the exact number
impossible to document.

## Plastic Paradise

Riding this rapid rise in home prices and subsequent borrowing
boom, credit card companies flooded Middle Class mailboxes with offers.  At the height of this frenzy, families with average income and a decent credit score might get an offer to borrow $100,000 on their credit
card with no fee at Zero percent interest for a year or more.

Many rationalized borrowing such an amount with the belief that
they could put it in the bank at five percent interest, and pay it back
after a year while pocketing thousands in bank interest.

But seductive lenders were betting that such money will "burn a hole in most people's pockets," that borrowers will spend at least part of it, be unable to repay in full, and get stuck with high credit card interest rates.

Many spent their home equity loans speculating on future stock increases. Was this what fueled the rise to more than 14,000 on the stock market?

Home equity lenders stood to gain a valuable house if their borrowers defaulted, or to earn reasonable interest if they did not.

Many homeowners, of course, fell into the trap of borrowing on one credit card to pay down another. For many this became a downward spiral of debt that devoured or cratered their American dream.

What kept this pattern of debt growing, of course, was that housing prices kept rising.

## Walk-away Ninjas

This meant that available equity kept increasing against which one could borrow. Having Fannie Mae and Freddie Mac as well as Nixonian inflation pouring liquidity into the housing market for a time kept home prices rising as more buyer dollars meant it took ever-more dollars to buy a house.

A joker has been dealt into the new version of this game. Because of the Carter-Clinton CRA rules forcing banks to give Ninja mortgages to millions of low income and minority home buyers, the once-stable cornerstone of the American housing market no longer exists.

Many Ninja buyers had taken out variable interest loans. If interest rates rose even slightly, these borrowers found it either difficult or inconvenient to make mortgage payments.

Because many Ninja borrowers had never been required to make any down payment to get into their homes, they had no real equity to lose.

If the monthly mortgage payment went up or their house value fell below the amount owed on it, millions of these Ninjas simply walked away in a move called "strategic default."

President Obama implemented policies that twisted the arms of lenders to reduce loan principal and monthly payments for such Ninjas.

Mr. Obama predicted that up to four million endangered homeowners would take advantage of his generous Home Affordable Modification Program (HAMP).

As of September 2010 fewer than 500,000 mortgages had been modified under HAMP, and of those who agreed to its new, even more favorable terms, fully half stopped paying again within six months. Lenders are now being squeezed to halt foreclosures.

Middle Class people would hesitate to ruin their credit by doing this. But underclass Americans seemed to have no such concerns.

Uncle Sam had given these Ninjas a home even though they had no income, no job, no assets and hence no solid credit record.

The Ninjas understood that Obama and the Democratic Party needed them and, no matter how they behaved, would keep giving them taxpayer-funded benefits. Liberals have taught them to think and act like a privileged class, above the laws and ethical rules others are expected to follow.

## Addicted to Stimulus

To stimulate the housing market, President Obama provided taxpayer-funded incentives of up to $8,000 to buyers. This apparently did not increase the number of home buyers. It merely persuaded those planning to buy soon anyway to speed up their purchases.

This latest Obama stimulus offer for homebuyers ended in May 2010, and in the following months home sales fell by up to 27 percent. The same economic  rise and fall happened with Mr. Obama's car stimulus program nicknamed "Cash for Clunkers." Sales blipped up and then, when the stimulus ended, nosedived to record low levels.

Potential homebuyers are now inclined to wait to see if Mr. Obama offers another juicy stimulus before they buy. Such government tampering with the marketplace thus can do more harm than good, quickly addicting people to crave and demand the drug of government incentives.

Potential homebuyers are also waiting to see if recent mortgage rates in the four-percent range will soon change, up or down, or if housing prices are about to plunge another ten percent or more.

Nobody wants to buy a house, then watch its value sink another 20 or 30 percent.

Potential home sellers do not want to sell for too little, even if their loss of hundreds of thousands of dollars in theoretical 2006 value is only on paper. Many find it hard to acknowledge that they are no longer paper millionaires, that the bubble has burst and come back to Earth.

Would-be sellers awaken each morning hoping to find that the Great Recession was only a bad dream, and that the value of their home has magically returned to what it was five years ago.

## Homes in the Shadows

One huge uncertainty for buyers and sellers alike is the "shadow inventory" of homes effectively owned by banks and others, but not yet put on the market. This invisible inventory is estimated to be anywhere from 1.7 to 8 million homes.

Some banks apparently would rather have unlisted homes on their books at a relatively high asset value than dump them on the market and watch their value collapse. These banks, too, await a return to prosperity to offer these homes. But other banks are more willing than families to write off asset value, and these banks may soon begin unloading their house inventory.

If anything like 8 million homes were suddenly dumped onto the housing market, this surge in supply would send home prices crashing downwards through the floor.

To potential buyers, plunging home prices might appear to be returning to the 1950s, a buyer dream come true.

To owners and sellers with their life savings invested in their homes, this would be a catastrophe.

Already one in four homeowners in America is upside down in his or her mortgage, in many cases from buying or borrowing when home values were high and rising, or from using one's home as an ATM, a source of ready cash when this was easy.

These upside-down folks now owe more than their homes would sell for today. This means that, unless they are in a group privileged by CRA, no lending institution will give a loan more valuable than their home's value as collateral. Their home has literally become a kind of financial trap preventing a move to find work.

If the economy weakens further and unemployment increases, a new wave of foreclosures will come as more and more people lose their incomes.

Buyers, sellers and those who depend on prosperous homeowners to boost their enterprises are holding their breath, waiting to see what happens in the November 2010 election, impaled by uncertainty.

Those who wait for the government to bring their financial salvation should remember the three things one can always assume are lies – "The check is in the mail," "I *will* respect you in the morning," and "We're from the government, and we're here to help you."

"One of the things that government can do more effectively than any other institution is create uncertainty," writes economist Thomas Sowell in *The Housing Boom and Bust*, "simply because government decisions constrain everyone else's decisions."

# Part Three
# The Dollar
# Decline and Fall

# Chapter Five
# Decline of the Dollar

*"There does not exist an engine so
corruptive of the government
and so demoralizing of
the nation as a public debt.
It will bring on us more ruin at home
than all the enemies from abroad...."*

– Thomas Jefferson
Letter to Nathaniel Macon, 1821

Today's paper dollar is a faith-based currency.

Officially convertible to nothing, the U.S. Dollar has value only so long as people believe in it. This is why John Exter, who was a Fed board member and a Vice President of the Federal Reserve Bank of New York, called the post-1971 dollar "an I.O.U. Nothing."

Most of us have trusted those green pieces of paper. We accept them as payment for the third or more of our short lives we spend earning a living.

Our lives are denominated in dollars when we trust this currency to preserve, protect and defend the purchasing power of the fruits we labored so hard to earn.

Yet beyond our childlike trust, the only thing in any sense "collateralizing" the U.S. Dollar is the "full faith and credit" of the United States Government, which by law designates these pieces of paper as "legal tender for payment of all debts, public and private."

Today, therefore, the real question increasingly asked around the world is "How much credit does the U.S. Government still have?"

If you were a bank or a nation, would you see the United States as a borrower you would trust to repay whatever value you lent it?

Would you invest your life savings in a company that, like the United States, borrows 41 cents of every dollar it spends, and that already has debts so gigantic that economists have called them mathematically impossible to pay off?

## The "Bankrupt" Superpower

"The U.S. is bankrupt," wrote Boston University Professor of Economics Laurence J. Kotlikoff in August 2010.

The International Monetary Fund (IMF) announced America's bankruptcy in a July 2010 Selected Issues Paper.

Few except Dr. Kotlikoff noticed because the IMF wrote in econospeak, the obscure language of economists, bankers and fiscal bureaucrats.

"The U.S. fiscal gap associated with today's [U.S.] federal fiscal policy," wrote the IMF, "is huge for plausible discount rates" and "closing the fiscal gap requires a permanent fiscal adjustment equal to about 14 percent of U.S. GDP" (Gross Domestic Product).

"This fiscal gap," wrote Kotlikoff, "is the value today (the present value) of the difference between projected spending (including servicing official debt) and projected revenue in all future years."

Government revenue today is approximately 14.9 percent of GDP.

"So the IMF is saying that closing the U.S. fiscal gap, from the revenue side, *requires, roughly speaking, an immediate and permanent doubling of our personal, income, corporate and federal taxes* as well as the payroll levy set down in the Federal Insurance Contribution Act." [Emphasis added.]

This fiscal gap, writes Kotlikoff, "is the government's credit-card bill and each year's 14 percent of GDP is the interest on that bill. If it doesn't pay this year's interest, it will be added to the balance.... Our country is broke and can no longer afford no-pain, all-gain 'solutions'."

"In a short period of time," warned Kotlikoff in a September 2010 speech, "the Federal Reserve would have to print trillions of dollars to cover its explicit and implicit guarantees. All that new money could produce strong inflation, perhaps hyperinflation."

The only people refusing to acknowledge that our nation is bankrupt are President Barack Obama and the politicians today occupying the Congress.

In technical terms, of course, a government can always stave off its own bankruptcy by bankrupting its people to pay politician debts.

## Point of No Return

The non-partisan Congressional Budget Office (CBO) issued a report on July 27, 2010, titled "Federal Debt and the Risk of a Fiscal Crisis." The report's most likely fiscal scenario predicts that America's national debt is almost certain to rise above 62 percent of Gross Domestic Product expected by the end of 2010.

If today's trends continue, CBO calculates, by 2020 America's national debt will be almost 90 percent of GDP.

In their 2009 book *This Time It's Different: Eight Centuries of Financial Folly*, University of Maryland Economics Professor Carmen M. Reinhart and Harvard University Professor Kenneth S. Rogoff warn that this 90 percent debt level is usually the point of no return for countries; those whose debt grows this large almost always see their currencies and economies crash and burn rather than regain health.

CBO projects that if today's levels of government spending continue, the U.S. national debt will be close to 110 percent of GDP in 2025 and to 180 percent of GDP in 2035.

Such spending above and beyond national income, warned CBO, is simply "unsupportable.... unsustainable."

## Double Your Money

In 2009 the Federal Reserve Board, America's private ruling bank, quietly doubled the U.S. monetary base. This means that twice as many dollars could soon be available from banks to stimulate buying in today's shaken, cowering economy.

This move by the Fed might immediately have ignited inflation. Dollars, after all, are subject to the same law of supply and demand as potatoes or any other commodity. If twice as many dollars are suddenly available to buy an unchanged quantity of potatoes, then (all else remaining the same) buying a 10-pound bag of potatoes will soon cost more money. This phenomenon is called inflation.

As of September 2010 government data showed prices holding steady. Liberal economists warned that not inflation but deflation, falling prices, was the dragon government needed to slay.

This view that lots more government stimulation spending is necessary dovetails conveniently with the Big Government ideology of economists such as Princeton University Nobel Laureate Paul Krugman and President Barack Obama.

But others recognize that inevitable and terrible inflation will result from running vast numbers of dollars off the printing press. The immutable law of supply and demand has not been repealed.

## Fast Money

What drives inflation is not only the existence of more paper money, but also its velocity moving through the economy.

By summer 2010 several hundreds of billions of dollars in stimulus had been injected into the marketplace at the urging of ruling politicians eager to produce jobs and at least a temporary sense that the economy was improving before the November elections.

Like water poured onto dry desert sand, instead of flowing outward this stimulus money sank in where it fell and seemed to vanish. The billions given to banks were used to replenish losses on their books, shape up their balance sheets, and allow them again to pay fat executive bonuses.

Instead of being lent to needy businesses and homeowners, other stimulus billions provided to banks were used to buy government obligations that paid the banks significantly higher interest rates than they paid to get the money.

In effect, government was helping banks get richer with zero risk without needing to make loans to the private sector. This left the private sector starved for credit.

Mr. Obama's economic team and media allies blamed all this on certain banks that had to be given bail-out billions because they were "too big to fail."

So what was the Obama remedy?  Like his predecessor, President Obama facilitated the takeover of smaller institutions by bigger government-assisted ones, thereby making the "too big" even bigger and the banking marketplace even more concentrated and collectivized.

Liberal cynics have noted that when Fidel Castro overthrew the government of Cuba and imposed Communism, he did not need to "collectivize" the island's agriculture. This purportedly had already been done by a handful of wealthy sugar and tobacco capitalists, and this made the transition to Communist collectivism easy.

Would it be too cynical for conservatives to observe that President Obama likewise is using government power and money to shift control of America's banking, insurance and automotive industries into fewer and fewer hands, especially left hands?  Mr. Obama is thereby collectivizing our economy.

## Fed Fiddling?

The Federal Reserve Board, at least in theory, is supposed to be above politics. But is it?

In September 2010, with November midterm elections only weeks away, the stock market staged its strongest rally for that month in decades, rising by 640 points.

Democrats gleefully heralded this as evidence that the Great Recession was over, that investors felt confident with President Obama, and that better economic times would soon arrive.

But savvy market analysts such as Charles Payne, the founder and CEO of Wall Street Strategies/WStreet.com, noticed that market surges in September corresponded 90 percent of the time within minutes to auctions under POMO, the Permanent Open Market Operations of the Fed.

Payne suspects that the Fed may be providing billions of dollars at essentially zero interest rate to one or more of its "Primary Dealer" banks and securities brokers, which then direct that money through channels to purchase stocks with a leveraged buying power 10 to 30 times larger than the actual money amount borrowed.

The Fed, in other words, might have used one or more of its Primary Dealers as delivery systems for money bombs targeted on the New York Stock Exchange.

POMO has been called QE Lite, another means alongside Quantitative Easing (QE, described by cynics as just another way of monetizing the debt, generating money from nowhere) to create economic stimulus.

If Payne's suspicions are correct, then Brian Sack and his colleagues at the New York Fed might have been conjuring the September stock market rally by indirectly using Fed money to buy many billions of dollars worth of stocks.

If that happened, it raises serious legal and ethical questions. Was a Potemkin Village unreal market rally created to benefit incumbent Democrats facing reelection? Were certain company stocks purchased for political or other non-economic reasons? Were laws broken, given that under current rules and regulations the Fed is prohibited from directly buying stocks?

Which of the Fed's Primary Dealer banks or securities brokers were big players in the September market surges? The Fed currently has 18 such Primary Dealers, 11 of which are foreign-owned, and all of which can borrow vast amounts of money almost for free from the Federal Reserve Board.

## The Uncertainty Factor

Businesses now feel a terrible uncertainty about government policies, as well as about the possibility that the Fed is manipulating the stock market and other players in our economy. How much higher will their taxes be from a President and his ruling party that make no secret of their ideological disdain for capitalism? How much will Obamacare and other laws and regulations increase the cost of hiring additional employees?

How expensive will it be to cover growing energy costs or to comply with rules restricting or taxing emissions of carbon dioxide, the same officially "dangerous" gas that puts the fizz in soda pop and that each of us exhales with every breath?

Even the current left-liberal Congress refused to enact Mr. Obama's radical energy legislation. The President responded with a threat to have his Environmental Protection Agency (EPA) impose the legislation's rules via executive branch regulations.

Mr. Obama in August and September 2010 had his EPA threaten to impose draconian restrictions on pollution caused by industrial boilers, the making of concrete, and "dust" given off by farmers plowing their fields. He is threatening this vast power grab even though analysts project that the new rules could destroy 900,000 jobs.

Mr. Obama's dictatorial rules will also send food costs into the stratosphere because farmers, unable to prevent dust in the course of plowing, will simply have to pay crushing government fines and pass this cost on to food consumers. But this is precisely what left-liberals now want – to tax the American people via capitalist intermediaries, so that government gets the money while the politicians denounce businesses as "greedy" and "gougers."

The EPA, incidentally, was signed into law not by a Democratic president but by President Nixon.

With similar power-grabbing high-handedness, Mr. Obama, after a judge struck down as illegal his ban on oil drilling from the Gulf of Mexico to Alaska, defied the ruling and issued a new shutdown order.

The Obama Administration expropriated banks and insurance companies as if he were dictator of a third-world banana republic or, worse, a Chicago political boss.

He nationalized two automobile companies without constitutional authority, then closed down dealerships apparently based not on how successful they were but on the race and political party affiliation of their owners.

In the case of Chrysler, President Obama haughtily slapped aside the legitimate contractual legal claims of bond holders he denounced as "greedy" so that assets of the company could be given instead to his political ally and major contributor, the United Auto Workers union.

## Frozen Money

Faced with such uncertainties and repeated presidential circumventions of the rule of law, corporations prudently began conserving the green they otherwise would have spent expanding, buying new equipment and hiring new employees.

Like millions of families, these companies had learned the words of a song from the Great Depression – "If I ever get my hands on a dollar again, I'm gonna hold on to it 'til the Eagle grins."

By summer 2010 analysts estimated that companies were holding back at least $3 trillion dollars – effectively reducing that money's velocity and ability to stimulate the economy to zero.

American families returned to something scarcely seen for a quarter-century – saving. By 2010 families on average were holding on to more than six percent of their income – and economists were predicting that this rate would grow by at least one percent each year for a decade.

For liberal economists these rediscovered virtues of prudence and thrift are nightmares. The U.S. economy had been getting 71 percent of its Gross Domestic Product from consumer spending (made possible by consumer debt via credit cards and home equity loans) – and in this brave new liberal world, a dollar saved was a dollar unspent and un-sales-taxed.

Liberals are now looking down the barrel of what their great teacher economist John Maynard Keynes called "the paradox of thrift," that in the politically-manipulated marketplace favored by liberals, those who save their money instead of spending it undermine prosperity.

## The Great Stimulator

President Obama injected as much as $2 trillion of stimulus money into the economy.

The lion's share of Mr. Obama's benefaction went to multinational banks, insurance giant AIG (which in turn transferred tens of billions of these taxpayer dollars to foreign banks), and others he favored.

His largesse with hard-earned taxpayer money created a handful of jobs at a "green" Midwestern battery plant at a cost of $600,000 per job.

Two Los Angeles government departments got $111,000,000 in stimulus funds but, as the *Los Angeles Times* reported, "created only 55 jobs." The cost per job: more than $2 million.

Obama's stimulus spending "saved" the jobs of tens of thousands of state and local government employees, including many members of teacher unions that contributed generously to the Democratic Party, and was used to add more than 250,000 jobs to the Federal Government payroll.

While private sector workers have been losing their jobs, Mr. Obama continues to hire up to 10,000 new Federal employees every month.

By contrast, in September 2010 Communist Cuba announced that it will allow more capitalist entrepreneurs to buy and sell with few restraints, and that it will be firing 500,000 government employees.

Russia likewise has announced plans to fire 100,000 government bureaucrats.

The average U.S. Federal Government worker is paid in wages and benefits $123,000 a year, up 37 percent since 2000.

This is almost exactly double the $61,000 annual pay and benefits of the average private sector employee, whose compensation has increased only 8.8 percent since 2000.

This means that the Obama Administration plans either to tax the private sector more heavily or to print tons of money to pay for all these additional public sector employees.

It also means that if President Obama had done stimulus differently – by cutting instead of raising taxes on private workers and businesses – he could for about the same "cost" to government have created productive jobs for perhaps twice as many people in the private sector.

By taking his "boot off the neck" of private companies – a metaphor that has come repeatedly from the lips of Obama Administration officials – President Obama might have boosted economic growth and increased tax revenues for his government. He might also have lowered an unemployment rate that has been stuck above 9 percent almost from the start of his presidency, employment that was only 7.2 percent in December 2008 before he began frightening employers out of hiring.

Such "easing" of government constraints on private sector companies and jobs, however, might not have enlarged the government or turned millions of others into dependents hooked on 99 weeks or more of Big Government unemployment checks.

In this, President Obama continues the proud legacy of his political party.

President Franklin Delano Roosevelt's motto was "tax and tax, spend and spend, elect and elect."

President Obama's motto might as well be: "Tax and tax and tax, regulate and restrict, then tax and tax some more."

It is not easy to move forward when every step taken must always be with the left boot.

One conservative-libertarian translation of this: left-liberal government breaks your leg, then gives you a crutch and expects you to thank it with your votes. It taxes away your ability to be self-sufficient, then offers you a life of dependence on government. Such benefits, of course, are given with ulterior motives and often come with strings attached.

By 2007 fully 58.2 percent of the American population – nearly three of every five citizens – was already dependent on government for "major parts of their income," according to economist Gary Shilling.

With 84 million Baby Boomers beginning to come of age for Medicare in 2011 and for full Social Security benefits in 2012, Shilling calculates that the proportion of Americans dependent on government for major parts of their income will reach 67.3 percent – more than two-thirds of our population – by 2018.

## The Baby Boom Goes Bust

Born from 1946 to 1964 as the children of World War II's returning soldiers, Baby Boomers have been our country's demographic "pig in the python," causing an overgrown bulge in maternity wards, then public schools, then colleges, then the job market, then the housing market, and soon in retirement homes. Eventually Boomers will overflow our cemeteries.

Starting in 2011 the Baby "Boom" will describe the sound of economic explosions in Medicare and Social Security as those underfunded Ponzi schemes are devastated by the sudden drain America's Largest Generation puts on their resources.

President Obama's healthcare law siphoning off more than $500,000,000,000 from Medicare to fund Obamacare is taking effect just as Baby Boomers begin to turn 65.

It seems to confirm a long-held fear of many Boomers.

After a lifetime of being taxed to fund these welfare systems, Boomers knew that when their turn came to collect from Medicare and Social Security as their parents had, the politicians who have diverted and spent the money from these trust funds and left only IOUs in its place would have to renege.

Boomers always suspected that they would be robbed by new rules that raise the retirement age or impose means testing to deny or reduce benefits to all who worked hard to have savings, pensions, a home or other assets.

And Boomers always knew that those who were irresponsible and profligate, and who lived as parasites on public welfare – turning the social safety net into a slacker hammock – will be given all the benefits denied to responsible Boomers who worked all their lives, scrimping and saving while paying high taxes.

Millions of Boomers whose investments have been lost to Mr. Obama's and the Democratic Party's Great Recession – or who will soon see their 401K or Individual Retirement Account (IRA) snatched away by liberal redistributionist schemes –  have resigned themselves to working until they die, to never being able to enjoy retirement as their parents did.

The only thing worse is to be of the post-Boomer generations destined to pay for the vastly expanded nanny welfare state and pleasure police that some liberals are eager to impose.

## Buying Votes

Mr. Obama's Big Government political party has a tremendous advantage. It has no need to persuade people to vote for ideas, or to bring diverse citizens together around values and principles.

Democrats win elections merely by promising to keep the government checks and free goodies coming, and by frightening their herd by accusing the other party of plotting to cut off those government benefits.

This is tantamount to offering people cash for their votes – but that, of course, would be illegal.

So Democratic Party politicians rely on the wisdom of Irish playwright George Bernard Shaw, who wrote: "A government which robs Peter to pay Paul can always depend on the support of Paul."

This is how we came to be ruled by the best government money can buy.

Those who recognize themselves as Peter in these politics would do well to remember another of Shaw's insights:

"You have to choose [as a voter] between trusting to the natural stability of gold and the natural stability of the honesty and intelligence of the members of the Government. And, with due respect for these gentlemen, I advise you, as long as the Capitalist system lasts, to vote for gold."

What does gold have to do with politicians robbing you? A great deal.

Liberal politicians still prefer a direct authoritarian approach to redistribution of wealth: rob the rich at tax-point, and give their wealth to precisely those poor who are the politicians' allies (while, of course, keeping a modest service fee of 80 percent or so for the government, as President Lyndon Johnson's War on Poverty welfare programs have done).

Note: this may sound a bit like the Robin Hood stories we were taught as children, but it is not. In those tales the evil Sheriff of Nottingham squeezed money out of working people. Robin Hood liberated this money from the Sheriff – the government tax collector – and returned it to its rightful owners.

Mr. Obama's party governs mostly by issuing decrees and passing laws designed to transfer money from the pockets of taxpayers into the pockets of Democratic voters and special interest contributors such as labor unions, trial lawyers, and bank and investment allies such as Goldman Sachs.

Like other modern left-liberals, Mr. Obama must squeeze money from voters who already feel robbed of their and their children's freedom and opportunity by too much taxation.

President Obama, therefore, is turning to inflation as the left's alternative form of mass wealth extraction. As Lenin told us, it is almost unnoticeable to a distracted electorate.

## The Hidden Agenda

Mr. Obama, an anti-capitalist ideologue, expects to get far more than money to enlarge the government out of the extreme inflation he has planned.

To understand his hidden agenda, we turn to a book written back in 1919 shortly after the end of World War I. This book, *The Economic Consequences of the Peace*, was written by the most influential liberal economist of the 20th Century, John Maynard Keynes.

"Lenin is said to have declared that the best way to destroy the Capitalist System was to debauch the currency," wrote Keynes. "By a continuing process of inflation, governments can confiscate, secretly and unobserved, an important part of the wealth of their citizens...."

"As the inflation proceeds and the real value of the currency fluctuates wildly from month to month," Keynes continued, "all permanent relations between debtors and creditors, which form the ultimate foundation of capitalism, become so utterly disordered as to be almost meaningless; and the process of wealth-getting degenerates into a gamble and a lottery."

"Lenin was certainly right," Keynes concluded. "There is no subtler, no surer means of overturning the existing basis of society than to debauch the currency. The process engages all the hidden forces of economic law on the side of destruction, and does it in a manner which not one man in a million is able to diagnose."

President Obama is unconcerned by the astronomical debts he is running up for a simple reason: he intends to liquidate them not with today's dollars but with a limitless quantity of new dollars he plans to create.

These new dollars will be created out of nothing on government printing presses and instantly inside Treasury computers. Mr. Obama will then spend them into the economy to buy whatever he wishes.

Because these new dollars are legally equivalent to your old dollars, these new bills will acquire their value by magically sucking the purchasing power out of the dollars in your savings account or stuffed into your mattress. The dollars you earn or have saved will lose value in this process. This is how government "taxes" citizens via inflation.

To leftists such as Vladimir Lenin, founder of the now-departed Communist Soviet Union, the greater value of such inflation is that it puts successful capitalists and those impoverished by their savings losing value at each other's throats.

Most people can easily be propagandized into blaming capitalists, who know how to survive and thrive and get richer in a hyper-inflationary environment, for their problems.

As Keynes credits Lenin for recognizing, inflation is so subtle and subversive that "not one man in a million is able to diagnose" that its real cause is government, the power that controls and manipulates the supply of paper money.

Inflation destroys the social cohesion and morality of capitalist countries. It is therefore a weapon and tool of revolution for socialists.

Could this be why President Obama almost rubs his hands together with glee as his policies devastate the American economy and each day bring America's weakening paper dollar closer to crashing?

## The Funeral Party

Americans have begun to understand how the rapacity of trial lawyers forces their doctor to practice defensive medicine by having them take many unnecessary and expensive tests – and that this has greatly increased the cost of health insurance and care.

Many Americans – thanks to talk radio, cable TV, the Internet, the Tea Party movement, and books such as this – are also now beginning to recognize that the mere presence of a political party that preaches class warfare and hatred for capitalism forces companies to practice "defensive business," to offer fewer services, do less investment, and hire fewer people than they would in a genuinely free market society.

All Americans pay a steep, invisible price every day in higher prices, unavailable products, and lost jobs and opportunity because the once-great Democratic Party founded by Thomas Jefferson has been taken over and subverted by radical anti-capitalist ideologues eager to turn it into the "funeral party" that puts capitalism into its grave.

Is this why President Obama is digging America into an inescapable deep hole of debt?

President Obama has already begun the fatal inflation of our nation's – and the world's – currency. A vast amount of stimulus money has already been borrowed or printed, and a lethal dose is being injected into our economy, with much more to come.

We do not yet feel its inflationary effects because trillions of dollars of this money remain frozen in the hands of banks, businesses and concerned citizens who are saving money, but are too uncertain of the future to spend it.

## Inflation on Ice

The Ancient Greek storyteller Aesop told the fable of a man who one winter day found a snake frozen in the snow. He carried it home and put it beside his fire to warm. But when the poisonous serpent thawed, it turned and gave him a fatal bite.

"Why," asked the dying man, "did you do this ungrateful thing after I saved your life?"

"You knew I was a snake when you took me in," the creature hissed in reply.

The frozen stimulus money injected to help win reelection for today's ruling politicians will soon thaw, and all of us will soon feel its bite and venomous inflation in the lifeblood of our economy.

For big-time borrowers this flood of paper money will seem at first to be a blessing, a way to pay off their reckless debts on the cheap with dollars worth far less than they borrowed.

For savers and lenders and those on fixed incomes, it will be a curse from the beginning by driving up prices and tearing down the value of each earned and saved dollar.

The torrent of inflation about to begin could soon kill the dollar and sink the economy for everybody.

This concludes this chapter's optimistic view of our economy.

Some analysts offer a far, far darker vision of where America, our dollar and savings, and the world are headed.

This is our next close encounter as we travel deeper into the Alice-in-Wonderland rabbit hole of Obamanomics.

# Chapter Six
# The Dollar Death Spiral

*"Paper money eventually returns
to its intrinsic value – Zero."*

– Voltaire
1729

*"There is no means of avoiding the final collapse
of a boom brought about by credit expansion.
The alternative is only whether the crisis should come
sooner as a result of a voluntary abandonment
of further credit expansion, or later as a
final total catastrophe of the currency involved."*

– Ludwig von Mises
Austrian Economist

At the heart of our Milky Way Galaxy is a giant black hole, according to scientists, a well of gravity sucking in and devouring the stars and planets around it.

These galactic monsters began as giant stars that suddenly collapsed in upon themselves, creating gravity so powerful that nothing, not even a photon of light, can escape their pull. This makes them appear black.

The edge of a black hole begins at what scientists call its "event horizon," the point at which to escape its doom a star or planet or photon would have to do what Albert Einstein's physics says is impossible – exceed the speed of light.

The U.S. Dollar, some analysts believe, is being pulled to its doom by inexorable and powerful political and economic forces. The dollar, some of these pessimists conclude, is close to – and may have already crossed – the event horizon, the tipping point of no return, at which nothing can overcome these gravitational forces.

Is the dollar's fate already sealed, its destiny to be hyper-inflated, shrunk to zero, and replaced by some new currency as happened to the dying money of Germany's Weimar Republic after World War I?

One of the most interviewed of such black hole economists is Egon von Greyerz, a former Swiss banker and now partner and analyst at Matterhorn Asset Management AG in Zurich.

Another is economic analyst Jeff Nielson, whose articles appear at, among other places, the popular investor website *TheStreet.com* founded by Jim Cramer and Marty Peretz.

We can start to focus on this alternative dark view of the dollar's future by examining it and today's U.S. and global economy through their telescopes.

## "The Dark Years Are Here"

The years 2011-2012, von Greyerz predicts, will be "the start of a long period of economic, political and social upheaval...."

The problems we are seeing, he believes, are symptoms of the collapse of the American Empire.

"All empires," he writes, "eventually overstretch their resources both militarily and financially."

The United States poured out its enormous wealth and the most patriotic of its young men in World War I, in World War II, and again in two wars against Communist forces that our troops were not permitted to win, Korea and Vietnam.

"But after the Vietnam war," writes von Greyerz, "the U.S. had overstretched its resources and by 1971 Richard Nixon abolished the gold standard in order to be able to start money printing in earnest.

"The money printing phase is normally the last stage of an empire before it collapses," writes von Greyerz, "and this is where the U.S. is now.

"The U.S. dollar became the reserve currency of the world when the U.S. was strong economically. But as the U.S. economy started to weaken in the 1960s-70s, the U.S. Government found a much better method for maintaining a strong economy.

"It started to print paper that it sold to other nations or exchanged for goods and services," writes von Greyerz.

"For almost 50 years this has been the most clever way ever devised of maintaining the living standards of an economically deteriorating nation without even having to spend any resources on building an empire.

"It is a Ponzi scheme which worked for several decades," writes von Greyerz, "but slowly the world is now waking up to the fact that they are holding worthless paper printed by the U.S. Government."

If the excesses of the 1970s had been promptly corrected, today's problems might have been fixed by 20 years of decline and rebuilding.

"But more likely," von Greyerz wrote in August 2010, "we will correct the era all the way back from the industrial revolution in the 18th Century, and this could take 100 years or more."

And what will this future of economic and social upheaval be like?

Von Greyerz answers in five stark words: "The dark years are here."

## Car Keys and Whiskey

Our fate and the world's was sealed, von Greyerz believes, the moment President Richard Nixon ended the last legal vestige of the gold standard.

(In 1933 President Franklin Delano Roosevelt almost completely terminated the gold standard, under which U.S. Dollars could be exchanged for a fixed amount of gold. Roosevelt also made it a crime for Americans merely to possess gold bullion without government permission.

President Nixon closed the last government window through which foreign central banks, not private citizens, had been able to trade in their dollars for gold at a fixed rate of $35 per ounce.)

Decoupling money from the firm anchor of gold removed the handcuffs that had prevented politicians from simply printing as much money as they wanted.

It gave them a credit card with no limit on how much they could buy and almost no political price to pay for using it to fund wars, buy votes or pay off cronies and allies.

"Giving government money and power," wrote journalist P.J. O'Rourke, "is like giving car keys and whiskey to a teenage boy."

## Burning Down Bretton Woods

President Nixon's action also effectively burned down Bretton Woods, the 1945 post-World War II agreement among industrial nations that set the exchange value of currencies relative to one another.

Bretton Woods was at least in small part based on gold pledged by its various members, especially the United States. In its schema, other nations pegged their currencies to the dollar, and the U.S. Dollar – at least in its dealings with foreign central banks – could be exchanged for a fixed amount of gold.

After Mr. Nixon broke with gold in 1971, the world's currencies were largely cut adrift to float, sink or swim and thereby find their own value levels in the global marketplace.

The United States Dollar was then, as now, the world's "reserve currency," the exchange medium through which commodities such as oil were priced, bought and sold. The U.S. Dollar was what the central banks of most governments stockpiled along with gold, a countercyclical hedge against inflation, to back up the value of their own national currencies.

Controlling the world's reserve currency and its availability and quantity gave the United States tremendous power. This made our money an "Open Sesame" in foreign trade, and made our credit almost golden when we wished to borrow abroad.

## Moneymaker to the World

America stood tall in the Post World War II world for many reasons – God's blessing, our moral values and reliability, and the fact that as home to people from all over the planet we continue to be the best example of how a united world could be. In every nation people have friends or relatives in the United States.

Two key reasons why America stands as a colossus are its legs – one of military might, the other of financial power.  We bestride the globe because these two legs work together.

Before Pearl Harbor, Japan's Admiral Isoroku Yamamoto implored his nation's military dictators not to attack the United States. He had been a naval attache in Washington, D.C., and understood that Japan had no hope of overcoming America's industrial might, our ability simply to make vastly more ships and aircraft than Japan could defeat. Military power throughout history has almost always been built from a foundation of financial power.

What price might we pay someday soon for having driven that industrial capacity and the jobs that went with it to foreign lands?

The Soviet Union collapsed after President Ronald Reagan challenged them with his Strategic Defense Initiative, mocked by our liberal press as "Star Wars."  The key to SDI was that it introduced huge uncertainty into Soviet military calculations about how reliably their missiles could strike us. Both sides knew that by spending each additional dollar, they could probably defeat two dollars spent on our defensive system. But the Soviets also knew that we were so prosperous that we could spend $5 or $10 for every additional dollar they had. Master chess players, they recognized that our money had checkmated their missiles.

The Gipper won, in part because Mr. Nixon had taken the lid off how many dollars America could spend on national defense. How ironic it now seems that the same money genie conjured from nothing to help us win the Cold War could soon destroy the world as we have known it.

## Fall of the Middle Class

"With no gold standard," writes economic analyst Jeff Nielson, U.S. bankers since 1971 have been "free to drown the world in their fiat-currency. Indeed, all inflation is a function of increasing the money supply; price inflation is merely the consequence of all that money-printing – as diluted currencies obviously and rightfully lose their value."

What this has caused, Nielson wrote at *TheStreet.com* on August 26, 2010, is the fast-approaching "collapse of...the dying U.S. economy."

"The combination of the collapse of the U.S. housing sector, massive unemployment, and the largest credit-contraction in the history of the U.S. economy," he wrote, have "combined to subtract approximately $2 trillion per year in consumer spending from this consumer economy."

Working Americans, Nielson has written, in dollars adjusted for inflation by economist John Williams of *Shadowstats.com*, now earn about the same as their great-grandparents did around year 1936 during the Great Depression.

The U.S. Government's Bureau of Labor Statistics in September reported unemployment at 9.6 percent. But according to Nielson and Williams, if older measuring techniques changed by President Bill Clinton's administration were used today, real unemployment is closer to 22 percent. Von Greyerz predicts that non-farm unemployment will within five years top 35 percent.

When so many have stagnant real wages or no income at all, it becomes impossible to sustain a consumer and service economy in which consumers create 71 percent of annual Gross Domestic Product.

Look around, says Nielson. Local shopping malls have many closed businesses. Without government spending, he writes, America would not be limping forward with 1.7 percent economic growth. We would have no growth at all, just frightened and angry Americans living on the last of their borrowed savings until the credit and the cash run out.

## "Go Big, or Go Home"

"The entire U.S. retail sector is in a terminal death-spiral," Nielson wrote, "and its only response is to eliminate vast numbers of retail outlets and herd consumers into more online retailing. While this cuts costs for these companies, most of those cuts will be reduced employment – fueling the next leg lower for consumer demand, resulting in even more store closures, etc."

President Barack Obama's stimulus measures have failed because they were billion-dollar "band-aids" trying to remedy trillion-dollar problems, wrote Nielson.

"The Obama regime has to 'go big, or go home,'" wrote Nielson. "It must either engage in massive (genuine) stimulus of the U.S. economy – meaning a multi-trillion dollar commitment, or simply allow the collapse to proceed (and feed upon itself)."

To do this, President Obama must confront "two other problems (which he created for himself)."

Mr. Obama and the Federal Reserve Board have propped up the U.S. Dollar, according to Nielson, by continuing "to pretend" that the U.S. was about to impose fiscal restraint and stop expanding government spending and debt.

## The Road to Hyperinflation

If the Obama Administration reverts to huge stimulus spending, this will erase any doubt among those who buy U.S. bonds and other obligations that he has chosen "the road that leads to hyperinflation."

This, in turn, could prompt China and other large creditors to stop lending us money, or to raise the interest they charge for such money, Nielson concludes. And that would leave President Obama only two options:

Mr. Obama would have to either create a crisis to frighten America's creditors to resume bankrolling our national profligacy on terms more favorable to us, or monetize our debts by running many trillions of devalued paper dollars off the printing press.

Mr. Obama's choice, as Nielson sees it, is either intimidation so we can keep borrowing money (albeit at higher interest rates), or hyperinflation from printing trillions of dollars.

Using devalued dollars to pay our obligations might be legal, but it would be seen by creditors as America defaulting on our debt.

This would be tantamount to the U.S. declaring bankruptcy and could make future borrowing either impossible or hyper-expensive.

Such behavior would also almost certainly mean the end of what former French President Charles de Gaulle enviously called America's "exorbitant privilege" of controlling the supply and distribution of the world's reserve currency – and the power, ease of credit, foreign trade and balance-of-payments security that, until the Obama economic crisis, came with this.

And as the dollar's death spiral ends in a fatal crash, American power, prosperity and security could be replaced by a new Dark Age.

## Doomsday Dollars

Even if the global economy of dollars somehow could be held together with chewing gum and bailing wire through the crises we face today, perils vastly more frightening lie almost unseen in the money universe's dark matter.

These mysterious time bombs waiting to explode are derivatives.

Remember how mortgages were bundled into packets and marketed for what often was more than their legitimate value, products that caused economic devastation in Iceland and wherever else these found buyers?

Behind these were various kinds of hedging agreements intended to reduce or disperse risk. These agreements, such as Credit Default Swaps (CDS), are called derivatives because they derive their value from some underlying thing of worth. Futures and options are also kinds of derivatives and have long been used in business.

As Bill Gross of PIMCO explains, fractional reserve banking allowed bankers to lend five or six dollars for every dollar actually on deposit.

Derivatives have given institutions such as AIG Insurance and others ways to create paper worth $10 to $20 for every dollar of backing.

During the 1990s and 2000s institutions churned out a significant amount of derivatives, which buyers snapped up as a way, they thought, to diversify their risk in investments. With the right derivatives, investors believed, they might lose a bit of profit margin but they reduced their margin of risk in many cases almost to zero.

What keeps investment from going crazy is risk. Risk makes people prudent and careful to watch where they step. But with derivatives seeming to erase risk, and with government promising to bail out all those "too big to fail," it became easier and easier for high fliers to wager on anything.

What they did not calculate was what happens if an economic collapse suddenly hits an insurer with so many claims that the insurer cannot pay off.

That, in effect, is what happened to companies like AIG – who pocketed billions for the safety promised by their insuring of derivatives but, when the great cave-in happened, was unable to pay out on hundreds of billions in claims.

Today the world's banks and other major financial institutions continue to hold years' worth of many kinds of derivatives – putting them on their books as if the derivatives have specific value. This bookkeeping allows banks to treat derivatives as assets against which they can borrow and lend.

How much are such derivatives – often very exotic, almost experimental financial instruments – really worth? Truth be told, this is a vast unknown in the flows of world money that the European and American "Stress Tests" of bank financial soundness have no ultimate way of testing.

Most derivatives are private contracts between parties that are subject to little or no regulation or oversight.

And how much asset value in derivatives is in the world's private and government banks and other fiduciary institutions?

Maybe this is why billionaire investor Warren Buffett describes these instruments as "financial weapons of mass destruction."

## One Quadrillion Dollars

The world's banks, governments and other institutions today hold derivatives worth between $500 Trillion and, in von Greyerz's best estimate, $1.28 Quadrillion – more than a Thousand Trillion – dollars.

Let's split the difference and look at the implication of the world's financial accounts carrying, as assets on their books, derivatives worth $750 Trillion dollars that might be worth only a tiny fraction of that amount – or, if push came to shove and they had to be sold during a world depression, might be worth next to nothing.

In our Introduction, we calculated that $4.4 Trillion could produce a stack of $1 bills from the Earth to the moon 238,857 miles away, with 59,753 miles to spare, enough to run a stack of dollars around Earth's equator 2.4 times.

By this yardstick, extrapolated from calculations by the business cable network CNBC, $750 Trillion would produce a stack of $1 bills that could reach all the way to the planet Venus, 23.7 million miles away at its nearest orbital point to Earth, and produce a second stack of $1 bills from Venus all the way back to Earth – and still have a stack of $1 bills 3.5 million miles high to spare for more than 14 stacks of dollar bills between Earth and the Moon.

By this yardstick, $750 Trillion could produce a stack of money from Earth to the planet Mercury 48 million miles away, with almost three million miles of dollars left over.

By this yardstick, $750 Trillion could build a stack of $1 bills to Mars 34.6 million miles away and have more than 16 million miles of stacked dollars to spare.

$750 Trillion could create a stack of dollars more than halfway to our local star the Sun 93 million miles away, even at Earth's farthest annual orbital distance.

$750 Trillion even in today's fiat dollars is an almost unimaginably serious amount of money.

## Zero

As described in our Introduction, Zimbabwe has printed $100 Trillion Zimbabwean dollar bills, single pieces of paper worth one-tenth of a Quadrillion of its dollars, as devalued by Weimar-like inflation.

"Paper money eventually returns to its intrinsic value – Zero," wrote the French wit Voltaire in 1729, a statement that von Greyerz has taken as his guiding motto in looking at the U.S. Dollar and other paper currencies today.

Derivatives are not dollars, of course, but they are held as valuable assets on the books of the world's major government and private banks.

The banks, having acquired them under various circumstances, cannot declare these pieces of paper worthless. If they did, the derivatives might have to be written off as a $750 Trillion loss, and this could cause many banks, perhaps including some government central banks, to go bankrupt.

In effect, these $750 Trillion of derivatives have become a new kind of money mostly kept uncirculated in locked bank vaults. If suddenly devalued, they could implode the world banking system whose accounts include them.

## Think of Them as Doomsday Dollars.

The world's other currencies, including the U.S. Dollar, would be unable to fill the value void that such a nearly-black hole-forming implosion worth $750 Trillion could cause.

Such an implosion is highly unlikely, state bankers would rush to reassure us. But most prefer not to mention their portfolios of derivatives at all.

Is this why President Obama's Security and Exchange Commission (SEC) in summer 2010 for weeks declared that it would no longer provide any documents requested under the Freedom of Information Act? A bipartisan outcry over such secrecy forced retraction of this policy in September.

One reason for this banker silence and government secrecy is that a big enough crisis could put pressure on banks to bring forth and liquify all their assets, including what could prove to be an astronomically large financial bubble of overvalued, worthless derivatives.

Derivatives are hybrid bets that, when called, could turn out to be an asset or a liability. This is why, in today's fragile economy, banks would prefer that they not be required to reveal what their derivates are actually worth.

For now, these derivatives are almost invisible and unnoticed dark bodies circling the same financial Sun that today's paper currencies do. But many have wildly erratic natures and unpredictable orbits that periodically cross ours.

Sooner or later they will begin to collide with and rain fire down onto our relatively tiny financial world, perhaps doing as much destruction as the six-mile-wide asteroid that scientists believe brought doom for the dinosaurs.

If and when that happens, we could be on the verge of a new Dark Age...as the vast hole of debt our politicians have been digging turns into a black hole.

## Knaves, not Fools

Because our dollar is the world's reserve currency and we are the biggest and richest consumer of the whole world's products, if the United States becomes a black hole we will probably pull the world economy down with us.

The Dark Years will spread around our planet and could eclipse the human future for decades, even centuries.

Smaller currency collapses have struck many times in history.

One of the most famous happened less than a century ago in the land that produced Albert Einstein...and, in part because of what hyperinflation did to society and individual morality there, produced the nightmare of the Third Reich.

Humankind today could be on the brink of the first global currency collapse, a potential breakdown of civilization with consequences that are terrifying to contemplate. If the dollar crashes and dies, other major currencies would likely then go into their own death spirals.

Politicians of both major parties have brought us to the edge of a cliff.

Earlier leaders may have been misguided or unlucky in moving the United States towards this dangerous place.

Today's rulers in Congress and the White House, by contrast, know exactly how close we are to economic destruction – but they keep piling on debt, weakening the dollar, and pushing us closer to the brink.

At what point do we admit to ourselves what has long been obvious – that these are knaves, not fools, and that they want to see the United States fall?

# Chapter Seven
# Crashing the Dollar

*"Theories abound to explain the President's goals
and actions....that Obama is clueless about business...
[or] something of a European-style socialist,
with a penchant for leveling and government
redistribution.... The real problem with
Obama is worse – much worse."*

– Dinesh D'Souza
Author of
*The Roots of Obama's Rage*

*"There hasn't been an empire in the history of mankind
that has given away its wealth and its power base
like the United States is currently doing....
You've got 20% unemployment. You're trying to
bail out the Chinese...Indians...the Middle East....
Why are you allowing this huge transfer of your wealth
to these other countries, who...are laughing?"*

– Philip Manduca
ECU Group plc, London
on CNBC, September 29, 2010

Voters are feeling buyer's remorse.

In 2008 they elected America's first Black president, an articulate and media-anointed comparative newcomer on the national political stage who promised a non-partisan, post-racial administration of harmony and good will.

President Barack Obama has fallen short of these promises, even his supporters admit, and has disappointed the best hopes of all who want our politics to be less polarizing and more inclusive.

Worse, Mr. Obama has spent most of his political capital pushing unpopular schemes that enlarge the government. He has been plotting massive tax increases on the "rich" while America has been burning down from the worst economic crisis since the Great Depression.

A footnote on President Obama's planned taxes: according to the National Taxpayers Union, as of September 2010 the top 1 percent of earners pay 40.42 percent of all income taxes; the top 5 percent pays 60.63 percent; the bottom 50 percent of earners pay 2.89 percent.

In 2008 voters also renewed the Democratic control over both houses of Congress by sizable majorities, reaffirming the switch in congressional power voters made in 2006.

During the first 19 months of his presidency, Mr. Obama and the liberal Congress increased the federal debt held by the public by $2.5260 trillion. As *CNSNews.com* editor Terence P. Jeffrey noted, this is "more than the cumulative total of the national debt held by the public that was amassed by all U.S. presidents from George Washington through Ronald Reagan."

We are rapidly plunging into a Debtocracy in which our future will not be governed by Republicans or Democrats but will be ruled and then ruined by an ever-expanding debt monster so large that it devours everything we, our children and our grandchildren earn and own.

We live, alas, in a post-laissez-faire world where people are no longer able to engage in voluntary exchange without government paperwork, taxes or interference. Today our government demands its cut, and often its say, in every human transaction.

We would be better off with separation of economy and state, but the government in general – and the left-liberals presently running it in particular – permit no such line of liberty to be drawn.

The military theorist Carl von Clausewitz said that war is the continuation of politics and diplomacy by other means. Today economics is all too often the continuation of politics by other means. Our politics and economy have become inexorably intertwined, so that to understand one we must examine the other.

## "Destroying the Country"

Daniel S. Loeb, a prominent hedge fund manager who, reported the *New York Times* on August 30, 2010, "has given and raised hundreds of thousands of dollars for Democrats," sent the following in a letter to his investors:

"As every student of American history knows, this country's core founding principles included nonpunitive taxation, constitutionally guaranteed protections against persecution of the minority and an inexorable right of self-determination. Washington has taken actions over the past months....that seem designed to fracture the populace by pulling capital and power from the hands of some and putting it in the hands of others."

Another major Wall Street investor and liberal, Stephen A. Schwarzman, was quoted in that *New York Times* story likening President Obama's tax plans to "when Hitler invaded Poland in 1939."

Ardent Democratic Party liberal Mortimer Zuckerman, the publisher of *U.S. News & World Report Magazine* and the *New York Daily News* wrote in August 2010 that President Obama is running "the most fiscally irresponsible government in American history."

Billionaire financier Zuckerman fears that Mr. Obama and the left-liberal Democrats who control Congress could be plunging the United States into "a long-term economic decline....a future of huge deficits or unprecedented tax increases, or both" that are "capable of destroying the country."

"Obama did exactly the opposite of what should have been done," said Nassim Nicholas Taleb, who teaches finance and risk engineering at New York University-Poly, in September 2010.

"[President Obama] surrounded himself with people who exacerbated the problem....total debt is higher than it was in 2008 and unemployment is worse," said Taleb, author of the best-selling 2007 financial book *The Black Swan*.

President Obama's bizarre response to America's ongoing economic crisis appears to be madness – unless some hidden method, motive or agenda lurks behind it.

## Smash Mouth Politics

Thomas Jefferson, founding father of the original Democratic Party, said that "great issues should not be forced on slender majorities."

To force major changes without broad public support, Jefferson knew, would lead to anger and discord, turning Americans against their government and one another.

Mr. Obama and today's Democratic rulers in Congress rammed through a government takeover of national healthcare, one-sixth of the entire American economy, with a tawdry parliamentary gimmick – "deeming" it to have passed so no new vote needed to be taken in the U.S. Senate after polls showed that a sizable majority of Americans opposed the legislation.

This brazen government expropriation of a huge segment of the economy was done not on a slender majority, but in defiance of long-established rules with no legitimate reconciliation vote whatsoever.

Had a recorded vote been taken, Obamacare with its astronomical costs and taxes, oppressive mandates on average citizens, and theft of $500 billion from Medicare would have lost.

If they had the votes to pass it, Democrats would have taken a vote. Because they lacked those votes, Democrats circumvented the rules to win.

When people in the rising Tea Party movement and elsewhere spoke out against this – or against any of a hundred other instances of high-handed White House or congressional smash-mouth political tactics and rule breaking – they were smeared by Democratic politicians and by liberals in the dominant media as "racists" who "just want to defeat a black president."

"We don't oppose President Obama because he's black," one talk show caller said. "We oppose him because he's red."

## Alien Obama

The first undeniable truth about President Obama is that he is culturally very different from any other president in our history. *Wall Street Journal* columnist Dorothy Rabinowitz describes him as "the alien in the White House."

President Obama is "a stranger in our midst," writes Robert Weissberg, Professor Emeritus of Political Science at the University of Illinois-Urbana, at *AmericanThinker.com*.

"[T]he Obama administration and its congressional collaborators almost resemble...a coterie of politically and culturally non-indigenous leaders whose rule contravenes local values rooted in our national tradition," Weissberg continues. "It is as if the United States has been occupied by a foreign power."

Perhaps the Boston tea party of the American Revolution era has inspired a political movement today, writes Weissberg, because Mr. Obama "subconsciously" reminds people of King George III, a German-speaking British monarch who neither understood nor respected the rights of Englishmen in the American colonies.

Jefferson's bill of wrongs committed by this king in our Declaration of Independence said: "He [George III] has erected a Multitude of new Offices, and sent hither Swarms of Officers to harass our People, and eat out their Substance."

Those offices, writes Weissberg, include more than 40 "Czars" empowered by President Obama to run government departments without traditional Senate hearings or assent. These Czars operate outside the longstanding system of checks and balances.

In September 2010 Mr. Obama named a Czarina, Harvard Law Professor Elizabeth Warren, to run his new consumer protection bureaucracy. He acted not only without congressional approval but also without Congress having control of her budget strings; this powerful regulatory office is funded directly by the Federal Reserve, a private entity, and thus can do whatever President Obama wishes entirely outside the traditional oversight and control of America's elected representatives.

## Pink Diaper Baby

Barack Obama's parents met in a Russian class at the University of Hawaii. His mother, from a radical-left activist family, had the counter-culture politics of a 1950s beatnik.

His father, Barack Hussein Obama, Senior, was a socialist and black nationalist from Kenya in East Africa who abandoned his family when his son was less than two years old.

Although President Obama is half Black, he is unlike most African-Americans because he has no American slave ancestors. His wife, and therefore his two daughters, do.

Barack Junior is therefore a classic pink (socialist), if not red (Communist), diaper baby who grew up in households where he first drank in radical thought at his mother's breast.

Young Barack reportedly was raised in Seattle and Hawaii, but when he was around age 5 his family moved to Indonesia, the world's largest Muslim nation, after his mother wed a citizen there. Barack, his childhood friends say, went occasionally to Mosque. He attended a school that taught Muslim prayers and recitation from the Quran, and hence could be deemed a Madrassah. He has said that the Muslim call to prayer is one of the most beautiful sounds in the world. Today Obama describes himself as a Christian.

By age 7 Barack was back in Hawaii living with his white grandparents. During adolescence his adult mentor and close friend Frank Marshall Davis was a poet and soft-core pornographer who wrote articles for a Communist publication.

## Rules for Radicals

In college, as Obama recounted in his autobiography *Dreams from My Father*, he sought out the company of "Marxist professors."

After graduating from Columbia University and Harvard Law School, Obama became a community organizer learning at the knee of radical activists in Chicago. He became a master of the tactics of Saul Alinsky.

Those familiar with the training manual *Rules for Radicals* – a book Alinsky dedicated to "the original radical...Lucifer" – recognize how precisely Obama applies its methods every day in how he attacks opponents and critics, and in the techniques he uses to advance his agenda.

(Hillary Clinton, incidentally, wrote her college thesis about Alinsky and is also a high adept in the use of his radical tactics.)

Mr. Obama later taught seminars in radical confrontation to leaders of ACORN, then represented this controversial community organizing group in one court case and worked as head of the Illinois branch of a voter registration group controlled by ACORN.

Obama began his electoral political career in the apartment of Bill Ayers, a founder of the radical-left domestic terrorist group The Weathermen, who on a legal technicality was found Not Guilty of involvement in a domestic terrorist bombing. Obama served alongside Ayers on the board of a liberal foundation. Some literary scholars have concluded that Ayers is the ghost writer of Obama's *Dreams from My Father*.

## The Pattern

Do such associations prove that President Obama is a hard-core leftist, a socialist or even Marxist? No. Nor does the adage "birds of a feather flock together" prove that Mr. Obama is a radical because he appointed self-described Communist Van Jones and other far-left radicals to high positions in his Administration.

The real question, to paraphrase the late William F. Buckley, Jr., is not whether Barack Obama is a radical leftist – but what would he be doing differently if he were?

If Mr. Obama were merely incompetent and making economic policy for our country by flipping a coin, then some of what he did by random chance would benefit the United States and the free market.

What is disturbing is that almost every single thing President Obama has done by policy and emergency decree neatly fits the pattern we would expect of someone who is trying deliberately and relentlessly to wreck the economy and crash the U.S. Dollar.

But the same can be said for the Democratic bosses in Congress, few of whom were pink or red diaper babies or radical community activists. So from where has this ominous pattern come?

## Changing Parties

Thomas Jefferson would not recognize, much less support, today's Democratic Party. The Democratic-Republican Party he helped found was very different. In fact, the Constitution makes no mention of political parties, despised as divisive, and referred to as "faction," by most of America's Founding Fathers.

Jefferson wanted a political party that put each state's rights above the Federal Government. Jefferson authored the original doctrine of "nullification," asserting that each state had the right to nullify specific Federal laws within its own border.

Jefferson favored the values of rural over urban America and viewed big cities as pockets of vice and corruption.

And Jefferson wanted government kept small and frugal. His "proudest boast" during his second term as President, he said, was that the average American "almost never sees a tax collector anymore."

Today's left-liberals always conveniently forget that the dominant theme in Jefferson is keeping government small. They are, for example, quick to quote one of Jefferson's private letters advocating a "wall of separation" between church and state.

When a modern left-liberal invokes the name of their god, The State, their syllogism goes like this: (a) church and state must be separate; (b) the state must dominate everywhere; (c) so therefore the church can express its religious views nowhere.

By contrast, when Jefferson referred to church and state, his syllogism was: (a) church and state should be separate; (b) the state, bound down by the "chains of the Constitution" must be confined to a tiny, tiny corner of the huge public square; (c) so therefore the church is free to express itself without government interference almost everywhere, and is separated from the state only to protect it from government favoring and funding one religion over others.

The next time liberals invoke Jefferson's informal idea of church-state separation, ask if they accept Jefferson's view that the government must be kept very, very small and limited in power.

Through most of the 19th Century the word "liberal" referred to people who favored free-market capitalism. Republicans emerged as the party of big government centralized in Washington, D.C.

## Southern Democrats

Democrats had been the party of Southern slave owners, but after the Civil War it became the party of the Ku Klux Klan, Jim Crow, and by the 1960s of Bull Connor and the Segregated South. Despising Republicans, Southern states voted solidly Democratic. With easy reelection assured in their one-party states, Southern Democrat members of Congress served many terms and, because of their seniority, chaired many congressional committees.

Southern Democrats were almost a third political party, differing in their cultural conservatism and strong support for defense spending from many Northern Democrats. But Southern states typically got back $3 or $4 dollars in Federal spending for every dollar they sent in taxes to Washington, D.C. They were the cornerstone on which FDR built the New Deal. The only Democratic Presidents in the 20th and 21st Centuries not born in the South or border South Missouri have been Franklin Delano Roosevelt, John F. Kennedy and Barack Obama.

By the early 20th Century, Republican President Teddy Roosevelt adopted many of the radical ideas of the quasi-socialist Progressive movement. After losing his party's nomination for a third term, he (like many of today's RINOs, Republicans-in-name-only) ran as an independent. By splitting the Republican vote in 1912 with his progressive Bull Moose Party, TR elected a fellow progressive, Democrat Woodrow Wilson.

Most Americans grew up thinking of Wilson as a New Jersey college professor from Princeton. In fact Wilson was born in Virginia, grew to age 14 in Georgia, and attended school in both North and South Carolina. His father, a Presbyterian minister, was a Confederate chaplain, and as a child Woodrow met and looked into the eyes of General Robert E. Lee.

As President, Wilson re-segregated government bureaucracies that Republicans had racially integrated 50 years earlier. Wilson also publicly endorsed the pro-Klan movie "Birth of a Nation."

During Wilson's Administration both the "progressive" (i.e., unequal) income tax and the Federal Reserve Board, with power to create and control the nation's money supply, came into being.

Wilson won reelection in 1916 with the slogan "He kept us out of war." Within weeks of beginning his second term, Wilson plunged America into World War I. He conscripted young men into the military. He also signed a law criminalizing "sedition," and used that law (much as John Adams had done 120 years earlier) to jail those who publicly criticized him or the war or the draft. He also effectively took America off the gold standard, thereby causing the Depression of 1920-21 that severe Republican budget cuts by economically free-market conservative Presidents Warren G. Harding and Calvin Coolidge cured to restore prosperity.

## Progressive Depression

Herbert Hoover was a progressive Republican who worked in Wilson's Administration, where massive U.S. food shipments he made to the starving Soviet Union saved its Communist government from collapse. As a RINO President, Hoover bungled the stock market problems that began in 1929, opening the way for progressive Democrat FDR to win the first of his four terms in 1932.

As British journalist Alistair Cooke reported, FDR brought America close to its own version of "national socialism," with gigantic government but little of Adolf Hitler's anti-Semitism. The New Deal failed to end the Great Depression here, while many other nations that left their markets free recovered rapidly.

Jefferson understood this perfectly. "Were we directed from Washington when to sow, and when to reap," he wrote, "we should soon want bread."

Yet this is precisely the kind of control that left-liberal Democrats from the New Deal to the present, with their smug sense of superiority, have sought to wield over agriculture, the environment, what foods we may eat, and everything else. And Obamanomics has so manipulated and damaged America's economy that we soon could have shortages of our daily bread.

## "Your Money or Your Life"

The same left-liberal Democrats who say the right will "impose its morality on us" never tire of imposing their own morality on others with what Obama ally Andy Stern, former head of the Service Employees International Union (SEIU), has called "the persuasion of power."

Left-liberals impose their morality not only via regulations but also by taxing away the fruits of your labor and transferring them to others, usually political allies, they deem more deserving of what you have earned than you are.

In the wild West stagecoach robbers would cry out "Your money or your life!" But in truth your money is your life. Each of us has only a limited number of hours on this Earth, and we exchange many of these – literally a large piece of our lives – to earn money for our families. When Democrats tax away more of our dollars to give them to cronies and political supporters, they are taking more and more of our lives that could have been spent helping our own children or fulfilling our own dreams, our own individual pursuit of happiness.

This expropriation of our life, liberty and pursuit of happiness violates our most fundamental human rights set forth in the Declaration of Independence. At what point does taxation become slavery?

## The Greatest Con Job

And speaking of slavery, FDR carried out one of the most amazing con jobs in human history. He persuaded African-Americans to abandon the party of the Great Emancipator Abraham Lincoln, the party that freed their parents and grandparents, and to vote instead for the party of the slave owners.

Democrats have mastered the divide-and-conquer politics of racial division and continue to use these tactics in 2010. Democrats favor different racial groups today, of course, but they still skillfully use racial preferences, polarization and hatred to gain and hold power for themselves.

By voting 95 percent for Democrats, African-Americans have nearly gotten themselves written off by the party that freed them, and taken for granted by the party that continues to enslave them with the addictive drug of socialist welfare programs.

FDR ended the gold standard for domestic currency that Harding and Coolidge had restored, and FDR in 1933 outlawed ownership of gold bullion for American citizens.

World War II ended the Great Depression. Vice President Harry Truman became President upon FDR's death on April 12, 1945. Truman then beat back a challenge by the new Communist Party-endorsed

Progressive Party candidate Henry Wallace, whom he replaced as FDR's Vice President on January 20, 1945.

Wallace, who described the Russian Revolution as part of humankind's "march to freedom," and who advocated embracing the Soviet Union, could be said to have come within 82 days of being president.

## Red Stalkings

The Communist Party USA received more than a million votes in American elections during the Great Depression of the 1930s. Its members became a target for U.S. Government surveillance in the 1940s and 1950s because they were unregistered agents of an enemy foreign power, the Soviet Union.

By contrast, America's Socialist Party was neither run nor funded from Moscow as the CPUSA was, and was not subjected to such scrutiny.

Was such surveillance justified? Carl Bernstein, who along with fellow *Washington Post* reporter Bob Woodward played a major role in bringing down President Richard Nixon, acknowledges quite candidly in his memoir *Loyalties* that his parents were radicals and secret Communist Party members. They, along with thousands of comrades, came to Washington, D.C., in conjunction with the radical ingathering of F.D.R.'s New Deal.

Surely it must be a coincidence that their red diaper baby targeted and brought down a champion of the anti-Communist movement in Mr. Nixon.

During the brief opening of the former Soviet Union's archives, researchers were able to document the accuracy of anti-Communist suspicions. The biggest surprise therein was that the threat of Communist subversives here was even greater than most anti-Communists feared.

It comes as no surprise that few former Communist Party radicals have apologized for conspiring to enslave their fellow Americans or for embracing a toxic ideology akin to Naziism that in the 20th Century killed more than 100 million people.

On those rare occasions when the left-liberal dominant media has acknowledged that someone was a Communist, it is quick to identify them as motived by "idealism," with no acknowledgement of the mass murder and bloodshed committed by their fellow socialists. Communism is no more "idealistic" than was fellow socialist Adolf Hitler's sick idea that genocide would lead to a better world.

## New Left, Old Left

During the 1960s and 1970s the left-liberal wing of the Democratic Party, which included many former Progressive Party supporters, was influenced by the New Left and anti-Vietnam War activists such as Bill Clinton.

Novelist George Orwell would think it ironic that in 1984 the Communist Party USA ceased running its own presidential candidates. From that year to the present, the CPUSA has directed its members not to break the solidarity of the left, i.e., to vote for the Democratic Party candidate. No Democratic Party nominee has ever publicly repudiated this Communist Party support.

The CPUSA's apparent motives for backing the Democratic Party may be fear of a Ronald Reagan-oriented Republican Party, or may be acceptance of a Democratic Party that has moved far to the left and over the years has put into law several of *The Communist Manifesto*'s ten measures to destroy capitalism and the bourgeoisie.

Among these measures proposed by Karl Marx and Friedrich Engels to kill capitalism are "A heavy progressive or graduated income tax" (check), "Abolition of all right of inheritance" (restoring the death tax, check), "Free education for all children in public schools" (because government schools will brainwash kids into believing that big government and its policies are good, check), along with "Centralization of credit in the hands of the State, by means of a national bank with State capital and an exclusive monopoly" (Federal Reserve, check) as well as "Centralization of the means of communication and transport in the hands of the State."

President Obama and congressional Democrat bosses are hard at work completing the implementation of these last two measures with laws to lock down the Internet and to control cable and broadcast networks such as MSNBC (which some say is a shortened form of Marxist-Socialist NBC).

They have plotted ways government regulators could require more left-liberal programs by radio and TV stations, and offered special tax breaks or government assistance to keep financially weak liberal newspapers and magazines from going out of business.

They have already seized many banks, controlled others with State capital, and expropriated two of America's biggest motor vehicle manufacturers, Chrysler and General Motors.

## Liberal Values

When you judge a tree by its fruit, some things become crystal clear about the agenda of President Barack Obama and his Democratic Party.

What objectives do President Obama and the left-liberals in Congress who have hijacked Mr. Jefferson's once-great party share, in addition to Democratic President Franklin Delano Roosevelt's guiding motto: "Tax and tax, spend and spend, elect and elect?"

Democrats favor redistribution of the nation's wealth from the successful to the unsuccessful, from rich to poor, from the productive to the unproductive.

This perennial modern Democrat policy uses class warfare designed to appeal to voter envy, jealousy and greed. It violates two of the Bible's Ten Commandments – Thou Shalt Not Steal, and Thou Shalt Not Covet.

And, as a bonus, Democrats give their voters a safe, legal way to rob their more prosperous neighbors and to pocket some of the swag that their liberal government steals.

## Banana Republican Democrats

Democrats favor a redistribution of political and economic power from the private to the public sector.

In keeping with this ideology, President Obama expropriated two of the world's largest carmakers, General Motors and Chrysler.

Mr. Obama then shoved aside Chrysler's secured bondholders, who under laws used here since America's founding had first claim on company proceeds, and instead gave 43 percent of the company's monetary value and 55 percent of its ownership to the United Auto Workers union. The UAW has been a major political contributor to both his presidential campaign and the Democratic Party.

After witnessing this, financial analyst Charles Payne called Mr. Obama's banana republic confiscation of property a "redistribution of wealth."

"What's going to happen the next time a company in trouble goes to get money from secured bond lenders?" asked Payne. "If they do, it's going to cost them a lot more."

Obama Administration "Banana Republican" Democrats continue to do interviews complaining that people and banks are holding back investment capital. Did they think people would rush to put capital at risk after President Obama tore up legal business contracts to enrich his cronies and political comrades?

One could devote 20 books of this one's length merely to document examples of how Mr. Obama and Democratic congressional leaders have put themselves above the law by their takeovers of American healthcare, banks, insurance and automotive companies, and other institutions.

And this is only the start of Mr. Obama's expropriation plans. What is his next takeover target? Your pension, IRA or 401K? Your savings account?

## Socialist Scofflaws

Although Democrats and Mr. Obama deny being socialists, the most common definition of socialism is a system in which "government controls the means of production."

After Mr. Obama's unconstitutional seizure of control over so many companies, what honest person can deny that this name fits what he has done?

Democrats have appointed a large share of America's judges. The mainstream media is also packed with their allies; an August 2010 survey found that 80 percent of political contributions from network producers, reporters and news anchors went to Democrats.

With these forces on their side, Democrats can manipulate the laws, suppress information about their high-handed behavior, and manufacture consent for what they have done.

When a judge rules against them, as one in Louisiana did against Mr. Obama's moratorium on ocean oil drilling, the Obama Administration has simply defied the law and continued its moratorium.

The Obama Administration put out a homeland security communique to law enforcement personnel nationwide suggesting that those who criticize the president should be put under surveillance as potential racists or terrorists.

In May 2009, after Arizona State University invited him to speak but refused to give him an honorary degree, President Obama in his speech there noted this refusal and said that the school's president and regents "will soon learn all about being audited by the IRS."

As investigative reporter John A. Andrew III documents in his 2003 book *Power to Destroy: The Political Uses of the IRS from Kennedy to Nixon*, past presidents of both major parties have used the Internal Revenue Service to harm as well as to gather information about media critics and others. Andrew shows how President Kennedy used the IRS to destroy conservative critics.

The 900 FBI files on Republican and conservative opponents used by President Clinton contained IRS records. Media critics such as Fox News Channel's Bill O'Reilly complained about incessant IRS audits he was subjected to during the Clinton Administration. The Clintons have reportedly urged President Obama to create an enemies list.

Whether or not President Obama has such a hit list, IRS audits will increase because this agency was made the chief enforcer of Obamacare, and because it will soon be building dossiers based on newly required 1099 forms each of us must file for every annual cumulative purchase of $600 or more. Mr. Obama is vastly expanding the IRS and its reach into everyone's lives.

Walk around Washington, D.C., and you will soon notice that all but one of the government agencies display eagles. The exception is the IRS, whose entrance is flanked by stone vultures.

It came to light in summer 2010 that liberal journalists were meeting on a website where ways were proposed to synchronize and coordinate media attacks against conservatives and Republicans.

Mr. Obama uses Chicago hardball politics to intimidate and silence those who differ with him.

## Calling Collect

Democrats favor transforming American culture from individualism to collectivism.

They promote policies to encourage people to think of themselves not as individuals but as members of groups, especially victim groups who deserve some sort of government reparations or compensation.

In Obamaworld you are supposed to think of yourself not as an individual but as part of a race, gender, ethnicity, economic class, or other collective group.

As a mere cog in such a collective, you must conform to its (pro-Democrat) ideology. Thus if you are an African-American, you are not to think for yourself.

Deviate and you will be called an "Uncle Tom" or a "traitor to your race," as former Ohio Secretary of State Ken Blackwell and U.S. Supreme Court Justice Clarence Thomas have been.

One African-American participating in a Tea Party gathering in St. Louis was savagely beaten by members of the SEIU. Local Democrat city officials have done almost nothing to pursue or punish his attackers, who like so many union goons in liberal cities are effectively above the law.

And such collectivism is not limited to earthly life. President Obama has repeatedly said that he believes in "collective salvation," that we are either all saved or nobody is.

## Demoncrats

This collectivist doctrine of Liberation Theology, repudiated by theologians of many denominations, in essence denies that your individual beliefs and behavior in this life make a difference.

In his 2004 book *Truth and Tolerance*, Joseph Cardinal Ratzinger – now Pope Benedict XVI – wrote of the fall of the Soviet Union that "... where the Marxist ideology of liberation has been consistently applied, a total lack of freedom had developed, whose horrors were now laid bare before the eyes of the entire world. Wherever politics tries to be redemptive, it is promising too much. Where it wishes to do the work of God, it becomes not divine, but demonic."

Mr. Obama's collectivist political and theological view is a central tenant of communism, socialism, national socialism (Naziism), welfare state socialism and other near-identical-twin collectivist cults.

All share the ideological dogma that the collective is everything, the individual human being is nothing, and each of us can and should be sacrificed without hesitation if this serves the interests of the collective.

# The End of History

Democrats favor locking in the changes they have made in American law and society so that these changes can never be reversed.

President Obama and Democrats in Congress know that they enacted Obamacare, a government takeover of one-sixth of the U.S. economy, in defiance of a solid majority of Americans reflected in public opinion polls.

Democrats know that they likely will lose their majority in at least one house of Congress in the November 2010 elections.

Frankly, if a private company's product carried such dishonest labeling, the Federal Trade Commission (FTC) or other agency would require that it be changed.

How can a political party that routinely acts in defiance of the will of the people be allowed to call itself the "Democratic" Party?

Someone should sue, demanding that it change its name to something more accurate and honest – The Socialist Fatcats Party, The Limousine Liberal Party, the Wholly-Owned Subsidary of Labor Bosses and Trial Lawyers Party, the Higher Taxes Party, the Gimme Party, something like that.  Your suggestions are welcome.

The FTC does not act here, of course, because when politicians made it illegal for companies to make false claims, they exempted and gave a license to lie to one group of people. Yes, you guessed it. They exempted politicians.

This is how Democrats can run in their home state or district claiming to be conservatives, then go to Washington, D.C., and declare that their elections are a mandate to enact hard-core leftist laws.

Politicians literally voted themselves a license to lie in their campaign advertising, and you are not allowed to sue them for breaking contractual promises to voters.

## Lame Duckocracy

So what will happen after election day 2010 if Democrats have lost their majorities in one or both houses of Congress?

However the people vote, Democrats will remain in power until at least January 2, 2011. During those months as Lame Ducks, Democrats can return to Congress and enact new laws free from the constraints that fear of facing voters gave them.

Democrat lawmakers who win reelection will not have to face forgetful voters again for two years or more. Democrats who lose may have this one last chance to vote with their looney left hearts and not their politically practical heads.

If Democrats lose their majority in November, some of them will see this as their last chance to impose legislation for years, even decades. They could decide to use these weeks to force into law as much of their ideological agenda as possible.

This Lame Duckocracy will be controlled by the same unpopular Democratic majority that, prior to the election, refused to pass a federal budget or take a recorded vote on whether to renew President Bush's expiring tax cuts – thereby concealing their real policies from voters.

With the election behind them, according to the Capitol Hill newspaper *The Hill*, Democratic leaders as of late September 2010 were already planning to take up at least 20 pieces of legislation in this Lame Duck session, some of which have remained secret in advance of the election.

One thing on the left-liberal agenda could be to ram through a European-style Value-Added Tax (VAT). A provision sneaked into Obamacare requires that purchases from any entity adding up to $600 or more per year will require the filing of an Internal Revenue Service Form 1099.

The purported purpose of this provision is to help identify those evading taxes via the underground economy, using purchases to flag those with greater-than-claimed incomes.

Financial experts have begun to warn that this lays the surveillance base that government can use to implement VAT as well as other confiscatory taxes and presidential Executive Orders. In our computer age, this tax policy could quickly become de facto government registration of nearly everything you own, from firearms to communication devices and wealth.

A lame duck session after this November's election could also produce heaven-only-knows what other laws – a huge tax on carbon? Gun control or confiscation? Political control over all agriculture, including back yard gardens? Censorship of the Internet? Amnesty and a quick path to citizenship and voting for illegal aliens, perhaps in time for President Obama's 2012 reelection?

Democratic lawmakers whose campaign funds have come from organized labor will support "card check," an anti-democratic measure that would replace today's secret ballot worker elections for unionization with individually-signed cards. This would give unions the ability to organize companies by having goons strong-arm or intimidate a bare majority of individual workers into signing cards.

A lame duck session could pass an endangered species law like what President Bill Clinton and Vice President Al Gore attempted. It would have expanded the Endangered Species Act to permanently include thousands of insect species. These species were carefully selected and would have given the Federal Government massive regulatory control – de facto ownership – of every square inch of land in the United States.

## Elected by Felons

The Democratic Party's operatives have long fought to restore the right to vote to convicted felons, including those still in prison. Why? Because, as you would expect with a political party that advocates robbing the rich, registration in the states where this is permitted indicates that felons would likely vote roughly 85 percent Democratic. Did anyone think Democrats would push to extend the vote to felons, or illegal aliens, if these groups were likely to vote Republican?

What would government be like if your elected officials won by courting felon voters? Can you imagine whose values they would serve in office? Or what laws might be passed to serve felons?

(To counter this movement: ask Democrats if they will also restore a felon's Second Amendment right to keep and bear arms.)

Democratic operatives also favor ensuring the voting rights of those in mental institutions, including those whose absentee ballots would be filled out and mailed in by government welfare workers.

A left-liberal lame duck session could also push national elections to imitate Oregon, where mail-in absentee ballots have completely replaced polling places. This gives members of the letter carrier union the power to decide whose ballot gets delivered for counting.

Although most letter carriers are honest, what would stop a few ideological zealots from going postal and destroying ballots sent from predominantly Republican neighborhoods? If such tilting of the vote in close elections produced 25 more Democratic members and a majority in Congress, voters would have no recourse to undo this before the next election, which could likewise be slanted.

## Santa Claus

Near the top of the Lame Duckocracy session after November's election could be illegal aliens and legislation to grant them immediate permanent resident status and access to welfare benefits, followed by quick and easy citizenship and automatic voter registration in time for Mr. Obama's 2012 reelection.

All these wonderous things and more could be rammed through and signed into law by President Barack Obama on Christmas Eve.

Many of today's socialist Democrats disbelieve in God – but, strangely enough, believe utterly and completely in Santa Claus, the tooth fairy, and the fantasy that America can tax and spend its way to prosperity by confiscating the capital from capitalism.

Once such laws are signed, they can be kept in place for two years by President Obama's use of his veto pen.  A new Congress, even with Republicans in control, will almost certainly have too few Republican votes to override presidential vetoes.

Even if the Democratic Party loses badly in the November elections, liberal lawmakers will take cheer, as Rep. Henry Waxman of Los Angeles already has, in their party moving even farther to the left.

Democrats most likely to lose are those who ran as conservatives in centrist districts.  By contrast, members of the congressional "Progressive Caucus," a  group of leftist lawmakers that used to be openly allied with Democratic Socialists of America, come from heavily-gerrymandered liberal districts where their defeat is almost impossible and they can be open about their extremist politics.

## Our Imperial President

President Barack Obama may be driven by something even deeper than a lust for power, the envy mainspring of socialism, or the pagan religious cult of Marxism.

Renowned author Dinesh D'Souza, the President of King's College in New York City, in his October 2010  book *The Roots of Obama's Rage* argues that our president became fixated on a missing father he remembers speaking with for only a few hours at age 10 and has made a lifelong crusade of his socialist father's anti-colonialist dream.

D'Souza, who grew up in India, writes that he recognizes these symptoms – widely seen in the third world – in President Obama's otherwise-bizarre politics.

Why, for example, was one of Mr. Obama's first acts as president to send back a bust of Great Britain's World War II Prime Minister Winston Churchill that had long been in the Oval Office as a symbol both of leadership and of our special relationship with the United Kingdom? Churchill is a great hero to most Americans, both for his courage and because his mother was American.

To Kenyans, notes D'Souza, Great Britain was a colonial oppressor against which Obama's father devoted his life. Obama's grandfather purportedly was demeaned by wealthy British who had expropriated African property. And Churchill was a hated symbol of the British Empire.

The United States, writes D'Souza, has replaced Great Britain as the world's great imperial power in the eyes of anti-colonialists – and hence in Barack Obama's eyes.

His eyes seem strangely blind to the historic fact that we were the first of Britain's colonies to win independence and inspire others. Mr. Obama could, if he wished, see the United States as a leader of global anticolonialism.

## Our Haunted President

From that ideological perspective, writes D'Souza, "America is now the rogue elephant that subjugates and tramples the people of the world."

This, writes D'Souza, is why President Obama has gone on a tour of the world, everywhere apologizing for wrongs the United States has supposedly done.

This is why Mr. Obama initially disparaged the idea of American exceptionalism and goodness, and why candidate Obama disdained wearing an American flag lapel pin.

This is why in Berlin Mr. Obama proclaimed himself a "citizen of the world," which should have disqualified him from seeking a presidency constitutionally limited to American citizens.

The irony in this, writes D'Souza, is that colonial empires are now in the past. "Colonialism today is a dead issue," he writes. "No one cares about it except the man in the White House. He is the last anticolonial."

"[O]ur President is trapped in his father's time machine," writes D'Souza. "Incredibly, the U.S. is being ruled according to the dreams of a Luo tribesman of the 1950s. This philandering, inebriated African socialist, who raged against the world for denying him the realization of his anticolonial ambitions, is now setting the nation's agenda through the reincarnation of his dreams in his son.... America today is governed by a ghost."

Is this the specter glimpsed by Christina Romer? The same specter of Communism that Marx and Engels said was haunting Europe?

Controversial as D'Souza's analysis may be, one cannot discount the potential impact of the formative influence that President Obama's socialist and anti-colonialist father's values have on the President's beliefs and policies today.

The pro-Obama intellectual media has gone berserk with attacks against D'Souza, especially in the wake of former House Speaker Newt Gingrich praising his book.

The gist of these attacks is scorn for the idea that a father Obama scarcely knew could shape his core beliefs. The ferocity of these attacks suggests that Dinesh D'Souza must be hitting close to the truth, a truth that left-liberals would prefer kept under wraps.

How else can we explain why Mr. Obama titled his precocious autobiography *Dreams from My Father* if his father had so little influence, or that he clearly seems to have adopted his father's socialist and anti-colonialist ideas? How else can we explain his insult to Great Britain by returning the Churchill bust? Why else is President Obama so hostile towards Israel, our ally, and so friendly towards the Muslim world that as President he bowed to the King of Saudi Arabia?

Why was President Obama so quick to shut down not just one leaking well in the Gulf of Mexico but virtually all offshore American oil drilling from Alaska to Florida in the name of environmental safety – but at the same time he is channeling $2 billion apiece to Brazil for deep ocean oil drilling, and to Mexico for its oil drilling in the same Gulf of Mexico?

## The Soros Connection

Another specter haunts American politics, the specter of multibillionaire investor George Soros, who decades ago waged a gambit that crashed the British Pound and reportedly shattered the life savings of many thousands of elderly Britons.

This eccentric currency manipulator, who has acknowledged having his own God complex, has poured hundreds of millions of dollars into helping elect Democrats.

His deepest concern, he has written, is the "Bubble of American Supremacy," the fact that America is the only superpower and is willing to use its might. According to Mr. Soros, this poses a great danger to world peace and security.

Soros wants the United States to be weakened so that it is no stronger militarily than, say, Germany or France.

In one thing Mr. Soros is absolutely correct – electing a Democratic President and Democrat-dominated Congress will, without doubt, make the United States far, far weaker.

His millions have played a major role in electing today's troika of left-liberal rulers over the American government, including President Obama.

If D'Souza is correct, then Soros and Obama share a deep ideological desire to bring down the United States as the world's sole superpower.

Mr. Soros made a billion dollars for himself by crashing the British Pound. Could he and Obama devise a coordinated effort to crash the U.S. Dollar?

The dollar is a global symbol of American wealth and strength that in its way stands much taller than did the World Trade Center twin towers destroyed by Islamist terrorist attacks on September 11, 2001.

Crash the dollar, the world's reserve currency, and you permanently cripple the power, prestige and wealth of the United States.

President Obama appears to be trying to crash the dollar. He and his appointees and congressional comrades have already added trillions in debt onto the U.S. economy. How might he do this?

## Socialism Evolves

Radicals with Barack Obama's kind of ideological background have had a game plan for toppling the United States for almost 50 years.

Socialists have developed several models for effecting such change.

In the 19th Century utopian socialists set up ideal communities such as Amana and Oneida, expecting the world to see their success and to imitate it. The names of these two utopias survive because, un-like hundreds of others that failed, these became known for making excellent products and turned into joint stock companies that made the no-longer-socialist children of the founders wealthy.

In the 20th Century Marxists fomented violent revolution to over-throw the old system with one blow. They failed in advanced societies, gaining power only in relatively primitive places like Russia, brought to its knees by World War I, and China, brought to its knees by World War II. Marxist dictatorship quickly spawned not equality but a privileged new ruling class even duller than the ones it replaced.

In the early 20th Century in England, socialists called Fabians, after the Roman general whose hectoring piecemeal tactics defeated Hannibal, created a successful piecemeal welfare statist takeover of the government. By relentlessly expanding the government a little bit here, a little bit there, they created a big enough class of state employees and welfare recipients to take over the government by ballot box.

"When the people find that they can vote themselves money," Benjamin Franklin reputedly said more than two centuries ago, "that will herald the end of the republic."

In the United States left-liberals from Presidents Wilson to FDR to Lyndon Baines Johnson, Bill Clinton and Barack Obama have used Fabian tactics to expand the welfare state, making it larger and more entrenched.

Capitalists have found ways to survive this swelling socialist tide, leaving many left-liberals frustrated at their inability to become all-powerful. They should have read Marx, who warned that overthrowing capitalism would be very, very difficult because the bourgeoisie is also a "revolutionary class," the class of Jefferson and Washington that over-threw the kings.

## Collapse the System

In 1966 two radical socialists at Columbia University, where Barack Obama would study a decade later, developed a revolutionary alternative strategy. Richard Cloward and Frances Fox Piven laid this out in an article titled "The Weight of the Poor" in the far left magazine *The Nation*.

Their strategy was to load up government welfare rolls with as many people as possible, then train them how to demand the maximum possible benefits.

The Cloward-Piven Strategy, as radicals from ACORN to Obama have known and used it ever since, is to overload, bankrupt and break the system.

In practice it is like that fad on college campuses during the 1950s and 1960s in which smart-aleck engineering students calculate how water flows in the school's sewer pipes, then have students in the dormitories synchronize the flushing of toilets to cause the system to overload and flood.

The sewer, having been designed to handle only light overloads, could have functioned without problem for 100 years, but is vulnerable to such deliberate sabotage.

The Cloward-Piven strategy likewise synchronizes demand to cause a welfare system overload designed to force politicians, and in particular moderate Democrats, to respond.

Whatever happens, from a radical socialist point of view this is a win-win situation. If Democrats rush to pour more money into welfare, they will then have to raise taxes on the Middle and Upper classes to pay for it. This effects a greatly increased redistribution of income to the poor and weakens capitalism.

Sooner or later, such increased taxation will eat up profits and end capitalism. Notice how in Obamacare insurance companies are mandated to provide many additional and expensive benefits, but are threatened with severe retribution if they attempt to raise their rates. This is calculated to drive private insurers out of business, leaving only government as the insurer of last resort, thereby creating the socialized medicine President Obama said he wanted in the first place.

In a Cloward-Piven mass attack on the welfare system, if politicians refuse to authorize all the benefits demanded, this then becomes a propaganda opportunity to proselytize those denied more benefits about their victimhood and the need to overthrow the capitalist system.

In classic Alinsky fashion, it polarizes people and sets them at one another's throats. It radicalizes many, making them useful pawns, weapons who can be directed by community organizers like Alinsky and Obama.

## Targeting the Health Care Dollar

President Obama is clearly using Cloward-Piven tactics to bring down the old cultural, political and economic order.

Under Obamacare, health insurance companies are already required to provide every customer with coverage for a vast new array of expensive procedures, including sex-change surgery and "children" who can now remain until age 26 on their parents' policies.

But the Obama Administration has warned health insurers that they will face harsh government retaliation if they raise their rates.

This essentially guarantees that private insurance companies, unable to make any profits, will drop out – leaving what Mr. Obama had said he wanted in the first place, a Euro-socialist single-payer government domination of everyone's health care.

He is already establishing new banking, financial, energy, agribusiness controls and taxes to do the same with these and all the other commanding heights of our economy, giving politicians the power at a whim to destroy or seize any private company or economic sector.

He has also taken steps that guarantee the collapse of America's whole economic system and the dollar.

## To Pay the Unpayable Debt

We have already reached a level of indebtedness that many economists say we will never be able to pay off. The interest on this debt will continue to dig us into a deeper and deeper hole.

Mr. Obama expended hundreds of billions of emergency stimulus dollars to keep government employees employed and to hire more – by some accounts an average of up to 10,000 new Federal employees per month, each with job security and a package of wages plus benefits twice as large as their counterparts in the private sector.

President Obama keeps stonewalling those who propose cutting government to reduce costs. He has flatly refused to go along with Eurosocialist welfare states Germany and France, who from hard historic experience in Weimar have chosen to fight the global recession with austerity measures, not massive new spending.

Instead, Mr. Obama keeps pressing for tax increases, despite the fragile state of the U.S. economy. In mid-September 2010 a financial analyst respected across the political spectrum, Mark Zandi of *Moody'sEconomy.com*, warned that if George W. Bush's tax cuts are not completely reinstated by their January 1, 2011, expiration date, the consequences will not be pleasant.

If these tax cuts end just for the rich, those families making $250,000 or more per year, by mid-2012 this will cut payroll employment by 770,000 jobs, raise the unemployment rate by almost half a point, and reduce America's real Gross Domestic Product by four-tenths of a percent.

## Crashing the Dollar

President Obama, in other words, cannot get the United States out of the current crisis by taxing the rich, and he refuses to cut the size and scope of the government he has been enlarging as rapidly as possible.

Every Obama Administration policy seems calculated in a Cloward-Piven way to keep putting pressure on the U.S. Dollar until only two options remain: to default on the U.S. debt, or to monetize the otherwise-unpayable debt by printing more than $100 trillion to pay it.

Default, like other forms of bankruptcy, would prompt other nations to demand payment in American assets – our oil fields, mines, property, and even the indentured servitude of generations of our taxpayers similar to the reparations imposed on Germany after World War I. Default would crash the dollar.

Monetizing the debt would trigger a Weimar-like inflation that will reduce the value of the dollar to zero. This, of course, would also crash the dollar.

If those are the only choices, then economists say it is better to wipe out the debt with worthless paper fiat dollars hot off the printing presses.

This would destroy America's economic, political and military standing in the world. Nations would stop lending us money, except at astronomical interest rates. We would be reduced for decades, and perhaps forever, to the status of a second or third rate power.

We would recover as a functioning society, but we would then be a former great power like Greece or Italy or no-longer-quite-so-Great Britain.

And by doing this, we could drag most of the rest of the civilized world down with us as their currencies and economies crashed, too. This could precipitate famine in vulnerable countries and wars in others.

# The Winners

Why would any ego-driven politician want to be remembered as the leader who ruined his country as well as others?

Mr. Obama does not identify with the United States. He is, by his own description, a "citizen of the world" – an anointed being whose divine destiny is to help abolish petty nations and usher in a one-world government.

To raise that global government up, the U.S. Government as the world's sole superpower must be torn down.

The person who does this will be viewed as a revolutionary hero by the new world order.

And since history is written by the winners, his winning collectivist side will make Barack Hussein Obama appear even better, brighter and more noble than he believes himself to be. He will be glorified as someone far larger in history than the leader of a single obsolete nation.

This, after all, is a politician who went out of his way to be photographed ostentatiously carrying a copy of left-liberal *Newsweek* editor Fareed Zakaria's 2008 book *The Post-American World*. This is the brave new world Barack Obama wants.

President Obama is not the slightest bit worried about the crushing debt over America's head. He expects it to fall like a guillotine on the neck of our independent capitalist system half a second after he removes his boot.

Mr. Obama expects our obsolete national economy and currency to be replaced by a new world economic order with global money that will wash away all old debts – except global taxes and reparations to America's victims – in the deluge.

If this leaves most Americans impoverished, so much the better.

That will make us utterly dependent for all necessities on the collective, to which we then must surrender our families and ourselves as serfs in the new world order.

What would a world in economic and currency collapse be like? To help prepare for what might soon be upon us, we next travel down the rabbit hole through time and space to a surreal economy where you will need a German dictionary – but we can live like millionaires with surprisingly few of that era's gold standard U.S. Dollars.

Get out your Passport. We are arriving in Weimar.

# Part Four
# Weimerica - Getting In, Getting Out

# Chapter Eight
# Next Stop: Weimar

*"Inflation is a disease of money."*

**– Jens O. Parsson**
**in** *Dying of Money*

*"Liberalism is just Communism sold by the drink."*

**– P.J. O'Rourke**
**Author**

Imagine you live in a world where politicians have just crashed the economy and money.

Whatever life savings in paper money people had put into bank accounts, stashed in a wall safe or stuffed into mattresses are now worthless.

Supermarkets and gas stations no longer accept either paper money or credit cards, but their last shoppers and first looters have already emptied their shelves and fuel tanks.

Roving gangs have begun raiding isolated homes and farms, and fear of soaring violent street crime keeps most people locked behind metal bars of their windows and doors.

All that most have left are things of now-uncertain value, like crystal vases or tableware, and a limited supply of survival essentials too valuable to trade away, like bottled water, canned food and bullets.

For most, their only items with barter value are a few pieces of precious metal such as gold wedding rings or other jewelry.

Less than 100 years ago a major European nation saw its money die and its society crumble into chaos just as soon could happen here.

We need to understand how this happened and how these people survived.

We need to prepare quickly for such a disaster not only here but also around the world, as some of the most powerful lords of finance have been doing.

## The Bankers Prepare

Millions of summer vacationers in 2010 escaped into vampire novels or murder mysteries.

But in England, many of the world's most powerful bankers were paying up to $700 apiece for rare copies of a 1974 book, reported the *London Telegraph*. In their elite inner financial circles of power and wealth, this was the hot summer's chilling best-seller.

This non-fiction book, *Dying of Money: Lessons of the Great German and American Inflations* by Jens O. Parsson, explores in frightening psychological detail how the debasing of money first seduces, intoxicates, confuses, surprises and then devastates people, nations and cultures.

Modern paper currency is what economists call "fiat money." Its only backing is a government declaration that it is legal tender for the payment of debts denominated in that currency.

Government makes no guarantee that its money can or will be convertible into anything – not gold or silver or even beans. At times in America's history the government has even refused to accept its own paper money as payment for its taxes.

These government pieces of paper we trust to store the labor value of our lives are, therefore, scarcely more secure or real than the paper "money" used to play the board game Monopoly™.

Money works only because people believe in it and agree to give it exchange value.

What happens when people begin to lose their faith in paper money, as sophisticated London bankers fear is happening to the U.S. Dollar and many of the world's other major currencies?

How low can the value of paper money fall when people stop believing in it?

Money's value can go to zero, as Germans learned to their horror in the early 1920s under the left-liberal Weimar Republic.

As bankers and economists know, the collapse of money in Weimar could soon occur again. And this time in our economically interdependent world a crash of the U.S. Dollar or the Euro could set off a domino effect, toppling one major currency after another and bringing down the worldwide system of money and trade.

A "global Weimar" is fast approaching unless today's policies change, the first President of the European Bank for Reconstruction and Development Jacques Attali warned readers of the *Wall Street Journal*.

Billionaire investor Warren Buffett has urged people to read another history of this horror, *When Money Dies: The Nightmare of the Weimar Collapse* by former Member of the European Parliament and journalist Adam Fergusson. This 1975 book provides details and descriptions of what it was like to live through a hyperinflation that could soon return.

By beginning with a look back at Weimar – how its hyperinflation happened, what damage it did, and why it suddenly ended – we might catch a glimpse of our own future.

We might also begin to see how to prevent, survive – and even profit from – the dying of today's money.

## The Great War

The Great War, as they called it in 1914, changed Europe and the world forever. This became the background for what happened in Weimar.

The war destroyed a world now scarcely remembered.

European geopolitics then was based on interrelated, intermarried inbred ruling families. The German Kaiser Wilhelm II's title, like that of his cousin, Russia's Czar Nicholas II, derived from the Roman imperial title Caesar. The Kaiser was a grandchild of Britain's late imperial Queen Victoria. In World War I, as it remains today, the British royal family is actually German, of the House of Saxe-Coburg and Gotha, that changed its name in 1917 to the House of Windsor.

The rulers of Europe's powers assumed that the war would end in quick victory and that their troops would be home by Christmas.

The war instead dragged on for four nightmare years that gashed the face and soul of Europe with rat-infested trenches and battlefields shrouded with clouds of lung-lacerating poison gas.

On the Allied side, almost 5.7 million Allied soldiers died. 1.6 million French troops perished and more than 4.2 million returned home wounded. Italy lost 1.2 million soldiers and suffered more than 953,000 wounded.

Nearly a million young men from the United Kingdom died in the war, and more than 1.6 million returned home wounded.

And like other European empires, Great Britain called on its colonies for troops. Thus into the vortex of devastation 74,000 soldiers from India, 67,000 Canadians, 62,000 Australians and more than 18,000 troops from New Zealand were pulled to their deaths.

More than 117,000 young Americans died, too – many of them drafted to fight as allies of the British monarchy from which we scarcely a century earlier had won our own war for independence and who unsuccessfully invaded the U.S. in the War of 1812.

Fighting with the Allies, the Russian Empire lost 3.3 million soldiers and watched almost 5 million return home wounded, many with missing arms or legs or eyes.

Uprisings in Russia against the war led to the abdication of Czar Nicholas II, the overthrow of the democratic Aleksandr Kerensky government, and a civil war that led to rule by Communist Bolsheviks.

To destabilize Russia, the German Government had helped arrange transportation for Vladimir Lenin from neutral Switzerland to Petrograd, thereby helping give birth to the Soviet Union. This would return to haunt Germany and cost millions of lives in World War II.

On the Axis side, the Ottoman Empire lost 2.9 million soldiers. Austria-Hungary suffered more than 1.5 million killed and 3.6 million wounded. The German Empire saw almost 2.5 million of its soldiers die and 4.25 million come home wounded or crippled or coughing from lungs shredded by mustard gas.

## "A Botched Civilization"

The Old Europe and its values were also fatally wounded on World War I's battlefields.

The Great War chewed people up in what seemed to be an unthinking machine of pre-drawn battle plans, knee-jerk responses and incompetent aristocratic leaders.

It was also a war of great patriotism in which the cannon fodder was not only flag-waving workers but also the children of the upper classes. Millions eagerly signed up to fight for idealism, chivalric knighthood, and duty to king and country.

Among the soldiers were millions on both sides who knew their Latin, having been taught to memorize the Roman poet Horace's words: *Dulce et decorum est pro patria mori*, "Sweet and fitting it is to die for one's country."

The flower of Europe, the cream of its best and brightest, saluted bravely and obeyed orders to charge into science's new-fangled machine guns, high explosives and poison gas. Some battles slaughtered more than 100,000 young men a day.

There died a myriad,
And of the best, among them....
For a Botched civilization....

Thus wrote the 20th Century American poet Ezra Pound, driven mad by what he believed happened in World War I and its aftermath.

## The Credit Card War

Many of the countries fighting in World War I assumed that they would win, and that as victors they would then compel the defeated to reimburse the winners' costs.

"Scarcely an eighth of Germany's wartime expenses were covered by taxes," wrote Parsson in *Dying of Money*. Instead, Germany "covered its deficits with war loans and issues of new paper Reichsmarks."

In other words, Germany fought World War I by borrowing and then running its printing presses, as did most of the other combatants on both sides. This is tantamount to paying for a war with a credit card. It provided immediate currency and, writes Parsson, avoided the political risk that overburdened taxpayers might turn against the war.

The only reason Germany could risk printing millions of Reichsmarks was that "a day or two before World War I opened...Germany abandoned its gold standard," wrote Parsson, "and began to spend more than it had, run up debt, and expand its money supply."

Great Britain, France, Italy and the other combatants also found ways to avoid honoring their own gold standards, which prior to the war would have given their citizens the power to exchange their national currencies for a fixed amount of gold.

A gold standard thus constrains those in government from printing money that the government lacks sufficient gold to redeem.

Five months after the United States entered the war in 1917, President Woodrow Wilson issued a proclamation requiring all who wished to export gold from the United States to obtain permission from the Secretary of the Treasury and the new Federal Reserve Board. Almost all such applications were turned down.

## The Health of the State

"War is the health of the state," wrote American social philosopher Randolph Bourne, who died of the Spanish influenza that swept the world killing an estimated 50 million people around the planet during World War I. This plague killed more soldiers than did all the battlefield bullets and bombs.

What Bourne meant is that a government in wartime can throw off many legal constraints on its power. It can impose martial law, conscript labor and soldiers, silence critics, confiscate property, and set aside a gold standard designed to prevent politicians from printing as much unbacked money as they wish.

(The modern version of this is President Barack Obama's former Chief of Staff Rahm Emanuel's mode of governing: "Never let a serious crisis go to waste....it's an opportunity to do things you couldn't do before.")

The Old Europe, knit together by an inbred aristocracy, proved deficient. A widely-repeated saying among British soldiers was that they had been "lions led by jackasses."

The gold standard for the most part had created prosperity and stability for decades prior to the Great War.

When all major currencies were pegged to gold, their value relative to one another was fixed and secure. And when wars had to be paid for with hard cash on the gun barrel, not credit or inflated fiat paper money, the gold standard was a powerful deterrent to war.

When today's liberals say they want a universal world currency and peace, these are what was lost when the World War I powers abandoned the gold standard.

What Mark Twain had called the "gilded age" had in many ways been an uplifting era, despite the difficult cultural transition from a civilization where most worked on farms to one where most worked in cities and factories.

## Making Others Pay

The Great War was devastatingly costly for Great Britain, France and the other Allies. But their politicians, as well as the families of those killed and maimed, at least had the consolation of being the winners.

These victors imposed a huge bill for reparations on the losers. As specified by the Treaty of Versailles, the Inter-Allied Reparations Commission in May 1921 decided that reparations owed by Germany were 132 billion gold Reichsmarks, then equivalent to roughly $31.4 billion 1921-valued U.S. Dollars.

"This was about four times Germany's maximum annual national product and greater than Germany's entire national wealth," wrote Parsson. "It was like asking the United States in 1973 to pay more than four trillion dollars in gold over a period of years."

One analysis found that paying off this staggering sum would have taken Germany until 1988, while another calculated that Germany would not have been free and clear of its reparations debt until year 2020.

(What actually happened was that reparations were suspended during the Great Depression and World War II, then payments resumed in 1959, and the reparations were officially paid off during a German reunification anniversary celebration on October 2, 2010.)

The victors at Versailles also stripped Germany of its extensive colonies and concessions in Africa and the Pacific, colonies not then granted independence but redistributed like booty among the victorious colonial powers.

Germany was required to surrender German-speaking Alsace and much of Lorraine to France as well, and, for a time, its coal-rich mines in the Saar.

Germany was required to pay reparations not only in money but also in millions of tons of coal and steel, foodstuffs, and even intellectual property such as the trademark for Aspirin.

As Germans saw matters, they had been forced into the war by Russia mobilizing a million troops on their ally Austria-Hungary's border and by France's refusal to agree not to attack their backs if Germany went to war with Russia.

Germany had already made a separate and advantageous peace with Bolshevik Russia in 1918 and ended the war with France and Belgium while its troops were still on their soil.

Germans found it difficult to understand why their leaders had surrendered. Adolf Hitler, who had been gassed as a battlefield foot soldier, joined other voices calling the German surrender the *Dolchstoss*, the "stab in the back" of Germany's "victorious army" by craven politicians, treacherous intellectuals and Jews.

Especially galling was that Germany was now to be bled dry paying reparations, almost as if they had become a colony of France, which they had defeated in the 1870-71 Franco-Prussian War and made to pay reparations to Germany.

## Ideological Upheaval

The German Kaiser abdicated in November 1918, and a struggle for power ensued. Marxists seized government buildings in Munich and declared a Bavarian Soviet Republic. Communist strikers in the Ruhr created a 50,000 strong "Red Army" to take power. Over three years various Communist rebellions struck Saxony and Hamburg.

Right-wing *Freikorps*, militias mostly made up of ex-soldiers, generally defeated Communist Red Guard militias that were inspired by the Russian Revolution.

"But for the nationalist armed intervention," wrote Austrian economist Ludwig von Mises, "Germany would have turned to Bolshevism in 1919."

Fleeing such violence in Berlin, a national assembly convened in the relatively tranquil town of Weimar. In August 1919 it proclaimed a new Constitution along Democratic Socialist lines. This affirmed labor, union and welfare rights and universal suffrage as decreed by the Council of People's Commissioners that ruled Germany briefly during the winter of 1918-1919.

This new Weimar Republic with its elected representative legislature, the Reichstag, positioned itself between the Communists, who wanted a Marxist-Leninist dictatorship of the proletariat instead of elections, and the rightists who wanted a return to the strong undemocratic rule of a Kaiser or dictator to restore stability and bring the left to heel.

"Between these two dictatorial parties there was no third group to support capitalism and its political corollary, democracy," wrote Austrian economist Ludwig von Mises. But in this time of crisis, he noted, it was capitalist entrepreneurs who imported the food and other goods Germany needed to survive.

(Kaiser Wilhelm II, ironically, opposed his "Iron Chancellor" Otto von Bismarck's plan to crush the socialists. Even more ironically, when Friedrich von Hayek wrote his classic book *The Road to Serfdom*, it was Bismarck's welfare prototype of today's Social Security that Hayek saw creating the levers of power a future Hitler could seize to create dictatorship.)

## Printing Money

All the great powers in World War I bankrolled their armies by printing money, taxing their people by thus inflating the currency that was no longer anchored to gold. Most also used a mix of rationing, patriotic peer pressure, and wage and price controls to reduce inflation's impact.

At war's end most returned to something like a gold standard, however, to put the brakes on such inflation. This sent prices sharply upwards. The United States transferred part of its gold supply to Great Britain to facilitate its return to a gold standard.

The U.S. now faced its own Depression of 1920-21, an event little noted in liberal history texts because it was cured by Republican Presidents Warren G. Harding and Calvin Coolidge tightening the money supply and cutting the size of government by 25 percent to wring inflation out of the system.

President Ronald Reagan likewise tightened the economy to exorcise his predecessor President Jimmy Carter's devastating inflation, thereby ushering in an era of relative prosperity from the middle-late 1980s through most of the 1990s.

During the Great War Germany had suffered inflation a bit worse than in Great Britain but a bit less than in France.

Germany's currency the Mark by early 1920 had fallen to "only one-fortieth of its overseas purchasing power" back in 1914, wrote Fergusson in *When Money Dies*. But in cost of living within Germany the Mark retained more than 10 percent of its 1914 purchasing power, and wages had increased to offset part of this loss by giving workers more Marks to spend.

The Weimar government made a fateful decision. Having lost the war, and burdened with crushing reparation debt, the government had little foreign credit left to keep the German economy afloat.

Germany's gold reserves had been largely depleted by foreign purchases during the war, and, if brought forth, its remaining gold would be demanded as payment by France and England. Returning to a gold standard under Germany's new democratic socialist regime was therefore unthinkable in 1920.

## Illusion of Prosperity

While other European nations and the United States slowed their printing of money, the Weimar government – eager for money not only to keep the economy running but also to expand its ambitious social welfare programs and the size of government – decided to continue printing paper fiat Marks at high speed.

Contrary to expectations, this flood of money at first was a tonic for the battered nation. While France, Great Britain and the United States faced the shock of going cold turkey off their wartime addiction to inflated money, Germany simply kept injecting paper money for its stimulative effect.

"Everyone loves an early inflation," wrote Parssons in *Dying of Money*. "The effects at the beginning of inflation are all good. There is steepened money expansion, rising government spending, increased government budget deficits, booming stock markets, and spectacular general prosperity, all in the midst of temporarily stable prices. Everyone benefits, and no one pays. That is the early part of the cycle."

This is precisely what happened during the early Weimar Republic. Factories were humming, and unemployment almost vanished. Food and beer were abundant, and incomes for a time rose faster than prices, which into 1921 were relatively stable.

As happens with all inflating fiat money, it was the illusion of prosperity bought on a credit card – and seemed almost miraculous, until the bills began coming due.

## The Morning After

"In the later inflation, on the other hand," wrote Parssons, "the effects are all bad. The government may steadily increase the money inflation in order to stave off the latter effects, but the latter effects patiently wait. In the terminal inflation, there is faltering prosperity, tightness of money, falling stock markets, rising taxes, still larger government deficits, and still roaring money expansion, now accompanied by soaring prices and ineffectiveness of all traditional remedies. Everyone pays and no one benefits. That is the full cycle of every inflation."

By late 1921 people began noticing that each Mark was losing value. The media acknowledged this, but blamed it on treachery and reparations paid to the French and English. Even much of Germany's financial world bought into this explanation for the weakening Mark, a confusion that would soon devastate the economy.

Looking back from 1975, Fergusson wrote: "The most notable thing about the puzzlement of the financial world, not the least the writers of the *Frankfurter Zeitung*, was complete failure to consider the continuing flood of new banknotes as one of the reasons for the mark's behavior (depreciation)."

Major business people endorsed the government policy. Hugo Stinnes, then the richest and most powerful industrialist in Germany whose empire reached across one-sixth of its economy, "justifed inflation as the means of guaranteeing full employment....as the only course open to a benevolent government," wrote Fergusson. "It was, he maintained, the only way whereby the life of the people could be sustained."

Yet as Fergusson notes, Stinnes built his empire in an inflationary economy that let him acquire properties on the cheap.

Later in the Weimar inflation, wrote Fergusson, the currency's "fall was reckoned disastrous for the finances both of the Reich and of the regional governments: all efforts to restore order in the federal budget had been rendered void. It meant the further impoverishment of the classes on fixed incomes, state officials included, and (as another newspaper feared) further recruits for the radical circles of the Right from the 'social declasses.'"

"What impressed the ordinary politician," wrote Fergusson, "was the danger of social unrest which would...inevitably arise if there were any scarcity of currency."

## The Unseen Connection

Most Weimar citizens simply failed to notice any connection between printing vast quantities of money and its declining value, just as today few Americans are facing the inevitable inflationary consequences of multi-trillions of dollars being thrown into the economy via partisan cronies by President Obama and our own Weimar-like democratic socialist ruling party.

Why were people in the Weimar Republic blind to what was causing their accelerating inflation?  And why did the early printing of vast quantities of paper fiat money not cause inflation instantly?

One answer is what economists call the velocity of money, the speed with which it moves from one hand to another.  More money by itself will not necessarily cause inflation if that money has little or no velocity.

Another answer, reported by both Parssons and Fergusson, is that many of the German people "clung to the mark, the currency they knew and believed in," losing their faith in it slowly. While the inflation grew, many naively still thought of their money as reliable, as good as gold, the way it had been before the war.

"We used to say 'The dollar is going up again'," a small Hamburg businessman years later told journalist and novelist Pearl Buck, "while in reality the dollar remained stable but our mark was falling. But, you see, we could hardly say our mark was falling since in figures it was constantly going up – and so were the prices... It all seemed just madness, and it made the people mad."

"The times made us cynical," his daughter told Buck, referring to the wealth  and opulent lifestyle of speculators and manipulators while Middle Class people sold off their possessions to them to survive. "Everybody saw an enemy in everybody else."

"The young and quick-witted did well," wrote one such cynic, Sebastian Haffner, in 1939. "Overnight they became free, rich and independent. It was a situation in which mental inertia and reliance on past experience was punished by starvation and death."

The first impulse for Middle Class Germans in 1920 was to hold onto any Marks they did not immediately need to spend, and this slowed down the velocity of the outpouring of paper money.

"At the beginning of an inflationary cycle," wrote Parsson, "velocity declines while money quantity increases, thereby offsetting one another and masking the true inflationary potential."

Inflation's illusion of prosperity can at first make people feel better able, but less pressured, to spend immediately.

This happened "in Germany's prosperous expansion of 1920," wrote Parsson, "....because money holders were temporarily willing to hold their excess money, slowing down velocity and leaving prices unchanged."

Astute readers will notice that we today face a frighteningly similar situation. Vastly more money has been injected into the economies in both the United States and Europe, but the velocity of this money has been slowed almost to a crawl by businesses, banks and citizens stashing their cash and neither spending nor lending a crucial inflationary increment of the new currency.

It is as if the private sector has tightened a temporary tourniquet to keep this dangerous inflationary drug from surging like snake venom through our economic bloodstream. But as with human beings, if the tourniquet is not soon loosened the tissues starved of blood will be injured or begin to die.

Today's fiat paper stimulus money soon will enter the economy, even though people in 2010 who have studied the Weimar hyperinflation must know the terrible consequences of such reckless spending by President Obama and his Congress-dominating Democrats.

## "To Smell a Government Rat"

The Mark's "Velocity started to rise with moderate vigor in the summer of 1921," wrote Parssons, "when Germans began to smell a government rat, and that signaled the gradual emergence of the latent price inflation."

Why a government rat? Parsson writes that he agrees with economist Milton Friedman that "inflation is always and everywhere a monetary phenomenon. No one can cause an inflation but the government, and neither more nor less is required to stop an inflation than that the government stop causing it."

"People's willingness to hold money can change suddenly for a 'psychological and spontaneous reason,' causing a spike in the velocity of money," wrote Ambrose Evans-Pritchard of the *London Telegraph* in an article about Parsson's newfound popularity with powerful bankers.

"Reichsbank officials were baffled," wrote Evans-Pritchard about Weimar. "They could not fathom why the German people had started to behave differently almost two years after the banks had already boosted the money supply."

The reason seems almost self-evident. If money is a reliable store of value, like gold, human beings tend to hang on to it. If money is unreliable as a store of value, then, wrote Parsson, "People naturally wish to hold money less and to spend it faster when they see its value falling."

As more and more Germans began to smell the socialist Weimar government rat, wrote Parssons, "Velocity took an almost right-angle turn upward in the summer of 1922," as people began spending their Marks faster and faster.

In Weimar as the inflation worsened, in part because of this accelerating money velocity, "Nobody wished to retain money," wrote Ludwig von Mises. "Everybody dropped it like a live coal."

According to von Mises, on the German Stock Exchange this behavior is called *Flucht in die Sachwerte*, "flight into investment in goods," the conversion of evaporating paper money into almost anything durable – gold, furniture, antiques – that will retain value better than a politician's promissory note, i.e., paper fiat money like Weimar's Mark or today's U.S. Dollar.

## The Money Trap

The Weimar politicians and Reichsbank by summer 1922 were frantically printing more and more money trying to keep ahead of the inflation they, apparently unwittingly, were causing.

In July that year the government passed a law permitting, under license, local and state governments and even large corporations to issue emergency money tokens to boost the money supply. These tokens, aptly enough, were called Notgeld.

Young writer Ernest Hemingway, then working for the *Toronto Daily Star* newspaper, went from France into Germany in the summer of 1922. "For 10 francs I received 670 marks," Fergusson quoted Hemingway as writing. "Ten francs amounted to about 90 cents in Canadian money. That 90 cents lasted Mrs. Hemingway and me for a day of heavy spending, and at the end of the day we have 120 marks left!"

After buying some apples, Hemingway was approached by an elderly gray-bearded German who asked how much they cost. "I counted the change and told him 12 marks. He smiled and shook his head. 'I can't pay it. It is too much.'"

"The old man," wrote Hemingway, "whose life savings were probably, as most of the non-profiteer classes are, invested in German pre-war and war bonds, could not afford a 12 mark expenditure."

Hemingway's five apples had cost approximately 1.6 Canadian cents. But this was only the start of the Weimar shift from high inflation to hyperinflation.

A liter of milk, which cost 7 Marks in April 1922, nearly quadrupled to 26 Marks by mid-September. The price of foodstuffs began to explode, despite bountiful harvests across the nation. Farmers were refusing to sell their foodstuffs for rapidly-devaluing Marks.

Soon German farmers began returning home from shopping or church to find that their livestock had been slaughtered and the meat hacked from skeletons and carried off by marauders. Theft and violent crime became commonplace in 1922-23 Germany.

Those on fixed incomes were wiped out by the hyperinflation. Men who worked hard all their lives soon found that their entire life savings could no longer buy a single postage stamp.

One analysis cited by Fergusson asserted that by 1922 it took a family of four 86 times as many Marks as it did in 1914 to buy the "minimum standard of existence," but in that period the average wage had increased by 34 times as many Marks.

## Golden Rule

For those who had gold or gold-backed foreign currency, Weimar Germany was a bargain-hunter's paradise. One American in 1923 Berlin tried to exchange a $5 bill for Marks but was told that nobody had enough Weimar currency to trade for such a huge amount of money.

Foreign exchange students, wrote Fergusson, "bought up whole rows of houses out of their allowances" that in their homelands were a pittance.

Speculators borrowed heavily to buy homes, factories or other valuables with bank loans, and then paid off the loans months later with nearly worthless hyper-inflated Marks.

"As the old virtues of thrift, honesty and hard work lost their appeal," Fergusson wrote, "everybody was out to get rich quickly, especially as speculation in currency or shares could palpably yield far greater rewards than labour."

As people's "financial and social position...slid away," wrote Fergusson, "patriotism, social obligations and morals slide away with it.

"The ethic cracked. Willingness to break the rules reflected the common attitude. Not to be able to hold on to what one had, or what one had saved, little as it worried those who had nothing, was a very real basis of the human despair from which jealousy, fear and outrage were not far removed."

Germany was suffering "the moral deterioration caused by inflation," wrote Fergusson. Many women succumbed to prostitution, and Germany became a favorite destination for both heterosexual and homosexual tourism.

## Cabaret

The Weimar Republic embraced Bohemian – later known as Beatnik and hippie – values, along with a wide range of what elsewhere were still regarded as sexually immoral "alternative lifestyles."

Perhaps the best popular image of what Weimar was about is the 1972 film "Cabaret," which won eight Academy Awards. Set in Berlin in 1931, it depicts the moral degeneracy of a society whose values and morals had been shattered by World War I and the hyperinflation that made fools of the thrifty, and rich people of those who speculated and borrowed. A central song in this musical is "Money Makes the World Go Round."

In the haunting final scene of "Cabaret," we see to our horror where all this "progressive" left-liberalism is leading. Uniformed Nazis who were laughed at and mocked early in the film have become a majority of the Bohemian nightclub's customers.

When the old morality and people's faith in their country is killed, and when as von Mises recounted "inflation had pauperized the middle classes" in Weimar, a national socialist cult of evil that blamed Jews and capitalists for everything that went wrong can become the new ruling faith.

## Weimar Leads to Hitler

"A straight line runs from the madness of the German inflation to the madness of the Third Reich," wrote German novelist Thomas Mann.

"The government calmly goes on printing these scraps of paper because if it stopped, that would be the end of the government," said Adolf Hitler in Bavaria, according to William L. Shirer in his 1959 book *The Rise & Fall of the Third Reich: A History of Nazi Germany*.

"Because once the printing presses stopped – and that is the prerequisite for the stabilization of the Mark – the swindle would at once be brought to light," said Hitler, showing a deeper understanding of economics than his fellow socialists in the Weimar government and Reichsbank.

"The state itself has become the biggest swindler and crook. A robbers' state!" said Hitler, a message that found sympathetic ears among many Middle Class Germans who already believed that their wartime patriotism had been betrayed, their life savings stolen, and their moral values mocked by the Weimar Government.

This gave Hitler a platform from which to scapegoat others for Weimar's devalued paper currency, called *Judefetzen*, "Jew Confetti," by German anti-Semites, and for Weimar's debasing of other social values.

The future Fuhrer's slogan became *Alles muss anders sein!* "Everything must change!" James Lewis of *AmericanThinker.com* translates this into what he calls "Obamalingo, 'Change you can believe in.'"

Hitler would later impose his own totalitarian socialist economics. He, too, eventually suspended the gold standard so that he could do unrestrained government spending by printing fiat paper currency of the sort he condemned during the Weimar Republic.

"Hitler instituted a New Deal for Germany, different from FDR and Mussolini only in the details" during the 1930s, wrote economic analyst Llewellyn H. Rockwell, Jr.

"Hitler's economists rejected laissez-faire, and admired [British economist John Maynard] Keynes," wrote Rockwell. "Similarly, the Keynesians admired Hitler" for using massive government spending to create full employment through giant public works projects such as the Autobahn.

"Perhaps the worst part of these policies," wrote Rockwell, "is that they are inconceivable without a leviathan state, exactly as Keynes said. A government big enough and powerful enough to manipulate aggregate demand is big and powerful enough to violate people's civil liberties and attack their rights in every other way.

"Keynesian (or Hitlerian) policies unleash the sword of the state on the whole population," wrote Rockwell. "Central planning, even in its most petty variety, and freedom are incompatible."

## 23 Skidoo

War reparations were to be paid in gold, not devalued fiat currency, and by January 1923 Germany simply declared that it could no longer pay. France and Belgium responded by sending troops to occupy the German Ruhr mining region. Germany responded by encouraging its workers to stage a work stoppage and show nonviolent resistance to the occupiers.

That same month the Reichsbank issued its first 100,000 Mark note. "Its purchasing power," wrote Fergusson, "equalled a little more than two dollars....a million-mark note was on the stocks and would be issued within another three weeks."

("Government is the only agency," von Mises purportedly once said, "which can take a useful commodity like paper, slap some ink on it, and make it totally worthless.")

By now many Weimar workers were being paid two or three times each day, rushing their pay to a waiting spouse who ran to buy what she could while money lost value literally by the hour.

"By the middle of 1923, the whole of Germany had become delirious," wrote Otto Friedrich in his 1972 book *Before the Deluge: A Portrait of Berlin in the 1920s*. "Whoever had a job got paid every day, usually at noon, and then ran to the nearest store, with a sack full of banknotes, to buy anything that he could get, at any price. In their frenzy, people paid millions and even billions of marks for cuckoo clocks, shoes that didn't fit, anything that could be traded for anything else," attempting to make their own *Flucht in die Sachwerte*.

People would order a cup of coffee at a cafe for 5,000 Marks, only to be billed 8,000 after drinking it because prices were rising so rapidly.

Fergusson noted stories of "shoppers who found that thieves had stolen the baskets and suitcases in which they carried their money, leaving the money itself behind on the ground." Others told of thieves who took wheelbarrows full of money who dumped the money.

U.S. Dollars were the most eagerly sought foreign currency in Weimar Germany. One group of seven party-goers recounted spending one dollar in Berlin in early 1923; after a large dinner and visits to "many nightclubs" trying to spend it all, the next morning they awoke to find unspent change in their pockets.

By the end of July 1923 a single U.S. Dollar was worth 21 million Marks.

Weimar's income tax was now rising by 25 to 40 fold per month, but the government depended on printing money for 99 percent of its revenue. In effect, inflation had become its preferred method of taxing the people, as it is for many left-liberal governments today.

Many Germans avoided paying direct taxes, rationalizing this as patriotism, as not wanting their money to go as reparations to the French.

## Marks to Market

By late 1923, 300 paper mills were supplying 150 printing companies that ran a combined total of 2,000 presses night and day to churn out the ever-growing flow of currency the Weimar government demanded.

On October 25, 1923, the Reichsbank declared itself a failure for printing only 120,000 trillion Marks when the day's demand had been for one million trillion! The bank announced that it would step up production to 500,000 trillion Marks per day!

The faster they printed, and the larger the denominations on each Mark, the less total purchasing power remained in circulation. The money's value was inflating away faster than they could print.

"Once begun, the inflation required ever more inflationary expansion just to support the old debts," wrote Parsson. "Germany had to run faster and faster to stay ahead of the engulfing wave, until it simply could not run any faster."

Parsson called this his "Law of Exponential Inflation."

As Ludwig von Mises described this insanity, the Reichsbank

showed an "Alice-in-Wonderland determination...to run ever faster in order to keep up with themselves." If only they had possessed Chairman Bernanke's helicopters!

With chaos closing in, on September 26, 1923, seven articles of the Weimar constitution were suspended. The socialist cabinet turned Germany into a military dictatorship to maintain national order.

Six weeks later Hitler attempted his failed beer hall putsch in Munich. He was arrested, convicted and sent to the jail, where he wrote *Mein Kampf*. Lionel Robbins in 1937 wrote that "Hitler is the foster-child of the inflation."

The Weimar Republic and German society were literally beginning to crumble like their currency.

Then something amazing happened that stopped the hyperinflation in its tracks and began to restore confidence and sanity.

To this day some economists use the word "miracle" to describe it.

Something similar might prevent or rescue the United States from the Obamanomics hyperinflation and worldwide Weimar catastrophe that could soon threaten our future.

Like the hard-pressed people of Weimar, you can survive and thrive during hyperinflation if you make wise preparations now.

We, as a nation or as individuals, can escape from the coming Weimerica.

# Chapter Nine
# Escaping Weimar

*"There are two ways to
conquer and enslave a nation.
One is by the sword,
the other is by debt."*

**– John Adams**

*"Germany will militarize herself
out of existence,
England will expand herself
out of existence, and
America will spend herself
out of existence."*

**– Vladimir Lenin
1917**

In 1923 Germany lay in economic ruins. The nation was bankrupt, deep in debt, and its currency the Mark was worthless.

Yet only 20 years later, despite the Great Depression and dictatorship by a genocidal madman, Germany had regained its former economic and military power. It had conquered France and much of the rest of continental Europe.

How did Germany survive and quickly recover from the Weimar Republic hyperinflation and currency collapse?

By October 1923 the old Mark had become ridiculous. Great Britain's Ambassador reported, even "a beggar would hardly accept any smaller note" than a million Marks.

## Neanderthal Money

A few small German states by then were pointing a way out. The Senate in Bremen began issuing gold notes. This new money, wrote Adam Fergusson in *When Money Dies: The Nightmare of the Weimar Collapse*, was "not in marks but in denominations of a quarter, a half and one dollar."

Bremen used the U.S. Dollar because in Weimar our gold-backed currency was then regarded as the most reliable and trustworthy on the planet.

The dollar originally got its name from the German Thaler, a precious metal coin widely circulated in the New World. The root word Thal means "valley," and reverberates today not only in our word dollar but also in the name given to ancient humanoids whose bones were first found in Germany's Neander Valley, the Neanderthals.

Bremen began issuing its gold dollar notes, redeemable after five months in government bonds or Reichsbank currency, in wage packets.

In October Bremen authorized a million dollars worth of its gold notes. And Hamburg, too, began to issue its own gold Mark notes

## Too Poor to Hoard

"Bremen took the calculated risk," wrote Fergusson, "...that the new gold notes would merely be hoarded. However, by the autumn of 1923, a new factor was at work – the absence of any ability to hoard."

Germans were too poor to afford the luxury of saving. Whatever money they were paid had to be spent immediately on necessities such as food.

Bremen officials gambled that their new gold-linked notes would produce "a fall in prices as retailers no longer had to allow for depreciation," wrote Fergusson. With a new currency that seemed to be gold-based like the pre-war gold Mark, merchants no longer needed to keep raising their prices by the hour to offset the hourly loss of value of dying Reichsmarks.

Bremen's positive results inspired the Reichsbank and national government to slow its issuance of more than 300 ten-ton railroad cars of worthless paper Marks that had already been printed.

German government spending by November 1923 reached six quintillion Marks – a six followed by 18 zeroes. By the following July, the number of paper Marks in circulation exceeded 1,211 quintillion. The old money had become a joke.

## Rentenmark Miracle

The national government and bankers decided to risk issuing a new note, the "Rentenmark." The German word *Renten* means "pension," with undertones of profit, income and revenue.

One gold-convertible Mark was now worth a million million ordinary Marks, the head of the Reichsbank announced, and a Rentenmark equalled one gold Mark.

Government and bank officials held their breaths, waiting to see if Germans would accept this value for the Rentenmark. The Finance Minister, noted Fergusson, compared this gamble on public confidence "to building a house beginning with the roof."

On November 20, 1923, after the old Mark had fallen in value during the previous five days by another 50 percent, the Rentenmark officially went into circulation.

Truth be told, Germany had too little gold left to convert very many Rentenmarks. The tangible backing for the new notes was not gold but mortgages on landed property and bonds on German industry, nominally still worth 3,200 million gold Marks.

"The Rentenmark was, in its literal sense, a confidence trick," wrote Fergusson. The real value of the mortgage guarantee behind it "was exceedingly doubtful, if not entirely illusory."

"The Rentenmark's own position was anomalous," he wrote. "It was not legal tender but, rather, 'a legal means of payment.' It was not convertible into gold, still less into the agricultural or industrial assets which were supposed to back it, although 500 Rentenmarks could be converted into a bond with a nominal value of 500 gold marks."

## Faith-based Money

The German people were exhausted and desperate for a new faith-based currency they could believe in, something that had a reliable value as their Marks did before World War I.

Most Germans embraced the Rentenmark not only as money but also as an anchor for paper Marks – that a million million fiat paper Marks were exchangeable for one Rentenmark, which was exchangeable for a bond worth one gold Mark.

This was a flimsy imitation of a restored gold standard, but it worked.

"The Rentenmark," wrote Jens O. Parsson in *Dying of Money: Lessons of the Great German and American Inflations*, "carried no real value of its own but the naked avowal that there would be only so many Rentenmarks and no more. The Germans miraculously believed it and, still more miraculously, it turned out to be true."

Inflation did not vanish overnight. The government continued to issue fiat Marks. But "the velocity of the circulation," wrote Fergusson, "slowed from a mad gallop to a sedate walk."

The greatest change was that farmers were willing to sell their goods for Rentenmarks.

"From the day of stabilisation onwards," wrote Fergusson, "there was at last the prospect that food might flow again back into the cities, and that one day the nation's budget might again be balanceable."

The hyperinflation fever had peaked and begun subsiding, thanks to the stabilizing power and promise of gold.

## Scars of Weimar

Yet that fever devastated the minds, souls and conservative values of millions of Germans.

The world saw its scars in Adolf Hitler's rise, legacy of anti-Semitism and the Holocaust, his ruination of Europe, and bloody downfall.

We see them today in the driven German work ethic and industrial success through which a nation flattened twice during the 20th Century, in World War I and its sequel World War II, has rebuilt itself yet again into one of the economic powerhouses of the world.

We also see the scars of Weimar's hyperinflation in those fearful Germans who cling to the welfare state like a security blanket, afraid to be self-reliant in a land where the Weimar collapse and other nightmares destroyed so many who worked hard and saved.

Such dependents of a paternalistic state, of course, are easily manipulated into shouting "*Sieg Heil!*" in Politically Correct socialist unison and doing the ruler's bidding.

Their road to security became what Nobel-prizewinning economist Friedrich von Hayek described in his book *The Road to Serfdom*, a road paved with the bones and blood of tens of millions of victims.

Most recently we feel the scars of Weimar in Germany's Christian-Democratic Chancellor Angela Merkel imploring President Barack Obama to learn from her nation's costly mistakes and to adopt austerity, not inflationary, measures in today's economic crisis.

Instead, President Obama has chosen the Weimar path of printing money, debasing the dollar, and taking on not only the risk of inflation but also of hyperinflation and the crashing of the dollar.

## Weimar Lessons

The Weimar Republic and its hyperinflation have much to teach.

They show the horror that can come from politicized money that politicians can run in literally unlimited amounts off government printing presses.

They show that inflation and hyperinflation can be both prevented and cured by money anchored in something as solid as gold, specified in the Bible as one of the few forms of honest money.

The ancient Chinese invented not only money but also paper money, which they called "wind money" because it could so easily be blown away.

Paper fiat money certainly fulfills one of money's two main roles – to be a medium of exchange.

Historically paper fiat currency has always failed to fulfill money's other main role – to be a dependable store of value.

The sad reality is that the greediest people in our society are not merchants or even bankers, but politicians.

Sooner or later politicians, craving money and the power that money can buy, will switch on the printing press to give themselves more to spend.

## Gold Haters

Most of humankind for thousands of years has loved gold for its beauty, its never-tarnishing incorruptibility, and its ability to protect the value of our savings in a compact, easily carried form.

Two groups of people, however, hate gold, at least when used as a standard anchor for national currency.

These gold-haters are modern politicians and central bankers. A gold standard prevents both from creating money out of thin air.

The reason for their hatred was laid out accurately in an essay by young economist Alan Greenspan, much later to chair the Federal Reserve Board. This essay appeared in Ayn Rand's 1966 book *Capitalism: The Unknown Ideal.*

"In the absence of the gold standard," wrote Greenspan, "there is no way to protect savings from confiscation through inflation. There is no safe store of value. If there were, the government would have to make its holding illegal, as was done in the case of gold" by President Franklin Delano Roosevelt in 1933.

"The financial policy of the welfare state," wrote Greenspan, "requires that there be no way for the owners of wealth to protect themselves.

"This is the shabby secret of the welfare statists' tirades against gold. Deficit spending is simply a scheme for the 'hidden' confiscation of wealth," he wrote.

"Gold stands in the way of this insidious process," wrote Greenspan. "It stands as a protector of property rights. If one grasps this, one has no difficulty in understanding the statists' antagonism toward the gold standard."

## The Wonderful World of Oz

Gold, therefore, clearly defines a fork in history's road.

Turn right onto the yellow brick road and it will lead you to stable money like that of the first 150 years of American history, when inflation averaged one-quarter percent per year or less.

That meant that money you set aside in the form of gold would retain its purchasing power for decades. This is the path to conservatism, prosperity and small government.

As Alan Greenspan wrote before becoming part of the current system, statists hate the gold standard because "gold and economic freedom are inseparable." These Big Government types despise economic freedom and therefore also loathe gold.

By the way, the yellow brick road also led to Oz, and that is no coincidence.

Some scholars believe that L. Frank Baum's 1900 tale *The Wonderful Wizard of Oz* is actually a parable about monetary reform in which the sure road is gold, Dorothy's slippers were in the original book silver instead of ruby, and Oz is the abbreviation for Ounce, the measure of gold and silver.

The story reflects the great debate of the 1890s in the upper Midwest,these scholars say, over whether government should issue gold-backed or silver-backed currency. This debate gave us 1896 Democratic presidential candidate William Jennings Bryan's famous "You shall not crucify mankind upon a cross of gold" speech.

Baum at the time was editor of a South Dakota newspaper in the midst of such populist activism, and his book was published in 1900, the year of Bryan's second presidential run.

## "Barbarous Relic"

Almost all modern politicians and their pet economists disdain gold as what statist economist John Maynard Keynes called a "barbarous relic."

To deconstruct what Keynes meant by such name-calling, he favored government intervention in national economies to smooth out the business cycle and redistribute wealth.

When economies were in the doldrums in the troughs of this cycle, Keynes wanted government to inject stimulus spending to spark economic growth.

When economies were at the manic peak of the roller coaster cycle, Keynes wanted government (or its central bank) to tighten credit and, in the words of one Fed economist, to "bring in the punchbowl" before the party became rowdy and disorderly....or, in the words of Fed chairman Alan Greenspan, to constrain "irrational exuberance."

Under a properly-functioning gold standard the economy is self-regulating and needs no government master to tighten or loosen credit or juice the system.

## Unnatural Economics

The business cycle will rise and fall, but this is the natural heartbeat of a living, growing economy based on the voluntary agreements of millions of human beings.

Liberals claim to be defenders of the natural environment but, oddly, want to impose unnatural controls and government manipulations to flatline the heartbeat of natural economics, i.e., the free market.

This, surely, is not the path to optimal economic health and well-being.

And neither is government redistribution of wealth from the makers to the takers in society, an unnatural movement of energy in the body politic from where it is productive to where it is unproductive.

Why won't left-liberals at least permit "free range" capitalism because this will produce a more natural, diverse economy? Why do they want free range chickens but tightly caged capitalism, i.e., a choke collar on free voluntary exchanges among mutually-consenting adults?

Will free markets have recessions? Absolutely, but these will tend to be shallow and end quickly as the markets are free to rebalance themselves. This clears out weak enterprises and redirects the flow of investment to stronger, healthier ones, just as happens in nature.

When government central planners try to improve the market, they intervene with limited knowledge and with outside political agendas to serve. Government is run by people who can screw up a one-piece puzzle.

## Control Freaks

Politicians of whatever political party are, for the most part, eager to control and squeeze maximum taxes out of the people. Such politicians, of course, want no limits whatsoever on their power.

For them, the power to tax means that government can never go bankrupt so long as it can bankrupt citizens with taxes in order to pay its bills.

A gold standard is precisely such a limit, as Greenspan wrote. It effectively prevents politicians like those welfare statist socialists who ruled the Weimar Republic from running the printing presses nonstop to give themselves more and more fiat money to spend.

And it prevents such politicians from using the inflation that this paper fiat money causes as a way secretly to tax those on fixed incomes and those with their life savings in dollars.

Yes, restoring a gold standard would prevent most inflation and all hyperinflation of our paper currency.

It would make spending decisions by all of us more careful and responsible.

It would create a fiscally honest society.

And for all these reasons, politicians of both major parties will fight to the last paper fiat dollar to prevent the restoration of a gold standard.

This is because a gold standard, as Greenspan indicated, would undermine the entire economic and political infrastructure of today's democratic socialist welfare state.

Excellent arguments can be made for various kinds of gold and alternative money standards, but laying them out would be a waste of time.

The reality is that so many politicians and others have a vested interest in keeping our fiat money system as it is that at least in the near term we will be unable to fundamentally change it except at the margins.

## Welcome to Weimerica

We already live in the launch stage of Weimerica, the reincarnation of the Weimar Republic, its morals and its hyperinflation, in America.

More than 60 percent of American households have at least one person living there who receives some sort of government benefit or payment.

The bottom 50 percent of citizens pay less than three percent of total income taxes, so to them the government is a free goody-dispensing machine for which they (wrongly) believe they pay nothing.

Approximately one-third of young Americans in a recent poll said that socialism is better than capitalism. Other pollsters find that far more young people support "free enterprise" than the left-smeared label "capitalism."

We have seen President Obama dump literally trillions of dollars of stimulus into the economy, only to produce an anemic growth rate in 2010's Second Quarter of 1.7 percent. This has done nothing to improve overall employment.

Mr. Obama could have produced more growth, of course, by using Fed Chair Ben Bernanke's helicopter to throw these same mountains of money into the air above random neighborhoods around the country. This, at least, would have given $4 trillion directly to the people, not special interests, to spend.

And, to be fair, President Bush began government stimulus policies by injecting $152 billion into the economy on February 13, 2008, almost a year before President Obama's inauguration. Mr. Obama has blamed his predecessor for everything that has gone wrong but never given President Bush "credit" for launching the policy of stimulus the Obama Administration copied and wildly expanded.

President Obama had other objectives than stimulating the economy for everybody. He channeled hundreds of billions of dollars to the giant banks and insurance giant AIG involved in causing today's crisis, and they have used all this taxpayer money to refill their own reserves and fatten their bonuses. Mr. Obama also generously spent money taxed from the private sector to enrich and enlarge government.

## Government Domestic Product

The silliness of today's Gross Domestic Product (GDP) growth numbers becomes clear when we ask one question: how much of the GDP comes from government spending?

Take a deep breath before reading the answer: approximately 43 percent of real total GDP is federal, state and local government activity, and if we added the financial activity caused by government mandates this number would increase. In September 2010 the Small Business Administration reported that one of every three dollars earned by private business now goes to comply with federal regulations.

This means that President Obama can make GDP grow anytime he wishes, simply by having government spend more.

The fallacy of government stimulus, of course, is that it must take the money from somewhere before spending it, and this taking prevents what would have been spending by private businesses and individuals. Keynesians have always justified this by claiming a "multiplier" effect for money spent by government – but the Great Recession appears to disprove the Keynesian claim.

Mr. Obama's policies, by both the uncertainty they cause and the inefficiency of his targeted use of spending and taxing to reward partisan allies and punish capitalist opponents, have slowed rather than accelerated the flow of money in America's economy. He and his congressional comrades created an anti-stimulus of businesses and individuals reluctant to spend.

GDP growth was impressive in the early years of the Weimar inflation, as new money surged into the economy and created the illusion of genuine prosperity.

This also means that without Mr. Obama's huge increase in government spending, America's GDP would be deep in negative growth. The left-liberal economists who in late September announced that "the Recession ended in June 2009" were saying this only to help Democratic candidates a few weeks before the national election. Or were they telling us that the Obama Depression began in June 2009?

And government creating 43 percent of our GDP means that we effectively ceased to be a free market country long ago. When higher taxes and spending shift another seven percent of GDP from the private sector to government, America will officially be a democratic socialist nation in which more than half of all economic activity is the state.

## First by Inflation

Abraham Lincoln said that in America the government is meant to be of, by and for the People.

The message from today's politicians of both parties is that you and your children will now toil your lives away of, by and for the government.

"If the American people ever allow private banks to control the issue of their currency," warned Thomas Jefferson, "first by inflation, then by deflation, the banks, and corporations that will grow up around [the banks], will deprive the people of all property until their children wake-up homeless on the continent their fathers conquered. The issuing power should be taken from the banks and restored to the people, to whom it properly belongs."

The Federal Reserve System, as critics describe it, is a private bank cartel. This analysis is laid out in economic historian G. Edward Griffin's 1994 book *The Creature from Jekyll Island*. The Fed has precisely the power to issue and otherwise manipulate the value of money that Jefferson warned of two centuries ago.

## Gold Standard D.I.Y.

The government is not going to restore the gold standard.

Asking politicians to consider this is a waste of time, as it is to ask them to end the "progressive" income tax. Few lawmakers or presidents of either party would give up these entrenched systems that give them so much power, revenue and ideological satisfaction.

The good news is that we can at least set up a gold standard in our own investments. Doing this kind of diversification is easier than you might think.

One of the biggest lessons to learn from the Weimar hyperinflation is that those who had gold or gold-backed foreign currency in Weimar did very, very well....and you can do likewise in emerging Weimerica, if you take steps to prepare now.

## The Dollar Trap

Whatever you decide to do, we recommend that you diversify your savings so that a portion – up to 25 percent – is put beyond the greedy, grasping hands of politicians.

Most people make the mistake of saving in dollars and dollar-denominated paper.

Today the U.S. Dollar is a fiat currency backed only by the promises of the same politicians who created today's economic problems, and by the debt those dollars represent.

Debt cannot be seen, tasted or touched. It, too, is like the ghost of the once-valuable U.S. Dollar. But the specter of debt can turn our hair gray, shorten our lives by causing stress, and – as President John Adams understood – snuff out the torch of Lady Liberty that used to enlighten our values and ideals.

Debt, like other addictive drugs, requires an ever-increasing dose for users to keep feeling the high that first stimulated and then hooked them. This produces a death spiral of ever-greater debt dependency.

"The problem with socialism," former British Prime Minister Margaret Thatcher reputedly said, "is that eventually you run out of other people's money."

Since socialist welfare states destroy the work ethic and drain the capital from capitalism, they always consume more of a society's wealth than they produce and, sooner or later, inevitably slide into economic death spirals, as European welfare states such as Greece have done.

When you invest your life savings in paper fiat dollars in our growing welfare state, you are buying the equivalent of junk bonds in a government with debts too large ever to be paid. You are betting your and your children's future on politician paper promises that can be made worthless almost overnight, as happened in Weimar.

Make sure that at least some of your savings have been converted from paper dollars into something solid – antiques, collectibles, stored food, gold – that will retain value when the dollar inevitably collapses.

To hold all of your savings in dollars is to stake your trust and future in the very politicians we all agree are untrustworthy.

This is a gamble no responsible grown-up would take, especially when it makes better economic sense to invest in things going up in value instead of dollars that continue to lose value and are politically being steered downward.

## Bipartisan Big Brother

The Democratic Party openly declares itself the party of ever-bigger government and government spending, the party devoted to government redistribution of America's wealth.

The Republican Party began in the 1850s as the party of centralized government power opposed to states' rights, and it has always produced its share of Big Government Republicans.

One of these was President Richard Nixon, who imposed wage-and-price controls, signed into law the Environmental Protection Agency and other eco-socialist schemes to undermine private property and business, and launched a dollar-destroying inflation spiral that continues today by severing the last link anchoring the dollar with gold.

The most recent Big Government Republican is President George W. Bush, who added a $40 billion drug benefit to Medicare, at the time the largest expansion of the Great Society welfare state since its founding in the 1960s by Democratic President Lyndon Baines Johnson.

To his credit, President Bush cut taxes but did so by agreeing to a law scheduled to sunset on January 1, 2011. He skillfully handled the national and global crises caused by 9-11 terrorism and prevented other terrorist attacks, but his military responses in Iraq and Afghanistan became the longest hot conflicts in American history.

Mr. Bush continued a world trade policy based on opening our borders and deliberately weakening the U.S. Dollar to make American export goods cheaper and more competitive in international markets. This keeps the dollar in a "race to the bottom" with foreign currencies trying to do likewise, and makes imported goods more expensive for American consumers. It is a de facto tariff that makes our dollar weaker and more likely to crash.

President Bush rushed in with $700 billion of government money in an attempt to prevent economic collapse in the emerging Great Recession and to prop up the heavily unionized automobile industry.

"I've abandoned free-market principles to save the free-market system," Mr. Bush told CNN interviewer Candy Crowley on December 16, 2008.

Voters often face a choice between a greater and lesser evil, between a Democrat politician eager to drive the economy off a cliff at 60 miles per hour and a Republican willing to steer the country over the same cliff at a more prudent 45 miles per hour.

What millions of us want are presidents and lawmakers who are serious about halting and reversing the growth of government and taxes.

## 9-11

On September 11, 2001, pilots followed established procedures when terrorists commandeered their airliners. Until then, such crazies had usually said "Fly me to Cuba," where passengers and crew stood a good chance of being set free with little harm. Pilots and crew were told to go along with such demands, that this would likely lead to less evil than fighting back.

By the time 9-11 passengers were being skyjacked eastbound across Pennsylvania, some had reached loved ones by cell phone and discovered that these Islamist terrorists were crashing planes.

At that point a few passengers realized that their airliner, United Flight 93, was headed towards Washington, D.C.

One passenger, Todd Beamer, had the courage to say "Are you guys ready? Let's Roll!" and with other heroes attacked and forced the terrorists to crash into an open field instead of the Capitol or White House.

Let's be brave enough to tell the truth here.

America has been skyjacked.

The Big Government crazies at the controls are not flying us to Cuba, turning us into just another impoverished socialist state.

It appears that they aim to crash the economy and the dollar, thus bringing down the global capitalist system.

They aim to bring about a "fundamental transformation" of the world in ways that will destroy everything America's Founders made, every individual freedom our Declaration of Independence and Constitution enshrined, every opportunity your children were supposed to have in a free society.

This November 2 we can vote to take back the controls from these power-mad crazies.

"The election in November is going to be one of the most important [in American history]," a former director of the New York Stock Exchange Kenneth Langone said on CNBC on August 24, 2010.

"If the American people continue the current makeup of the Congress, it's a formal endorsement of what's going on – and that would be scary," said Langone.

"I hope we get a resounding statement by the American people that this is not what we want. We don't want socialism."

"The Republican Party got drunk on debt, too," said Langone, who as a venture capitalist was co-founder of Home Depot. America needs to be "taking the cure...it's going to be painful."

The alternative is to leave our fate in foreign lender hands.

"The minute our foreign partners stop taking our debt, it's game, set, match...it's over," said Langone.

Pray that the election on November 2 changes things, and that those who win control in Congress have the courage and vision to block funding and implementation of what politicians have already unethically forced into law.

We need to reverse the flight plan programming for a Weimar-style crash that power-addicted politicians have tried to lock into America's autopilot.

We need to start returning America to the moral and sound-money course set two centuries ago by our country's Founders.

Let's roll.